THE GREAT REDUCTION

The Great Reduction

SOLOMON SEEKS THE KEY TO PEACE

Jay Trott

WIPF & STOCK · Eugene, Oregon

THE GREAT REDUCTION
Solomon Seeks the Key to Peace

Copyright © 2020 Jay Trott. All rights reserved. Except for brief quotations in critical publications or reviews, no part of this book may be reproduced in any manner without prior written permission from the publisher. Write: Permissions, Wipf and Stock Publishers, 199 W. 8th Ave., Suite 3, Eugene, OR 97401.

Wipf & Stock
An Imprint of Wipf and Stock Publishers
199 W. 8th Ave., Suite 3
Eugene, OR 97401

www.wipfandstock.com

PAPERBACK ISBN: 978-1-7252-6478-6
HARDCOVER ISBN: 978-1-7252-6479-3
EBOOK ISBN: 978-1-7252-6480-9

Manufactured in the U.S.A.   AUGUST 5, 2020

Acknowledgments

MANY THANKS TO THOSE who kindly read and commented on the manuscript, including Fr. James Wheeler and my wonderful wife, Beth. This book is dedicated to the glory of God.

THE GREAT REDUCTION

Ecclesiastes is a remarkable little book about how to find contentment—and how not to find it.

For my own part, I'm just now realizing that I have not been allowing Solomon to say what he really wants to say all these years. Seems the story I brought along with me kept drowning out *his* story.

But now I'm in pretty much the same boat he was in when he wrote it. I'm getting a little long in the tooth myself and trying to stay away from mirrors. And as a result, his amazing book is starting to come into focus for me in an entirely new way.

I'll call my story the *justice narrative*. It goes something like this: the just and the good are rewarded and the wicked get what's coming to them. Ecclesiastes is the antidote to that story. In fact it shows what happens when such stories fall apart—the devastating impact this can have on identity.

You'll remember Solomon as a younger man, full of his proverbs. The justice narrative was strong in him. But as an old man he has seen far too many things. The justice narrative has begun to take on water, and he finds himself casting about, a little desperately, for something to grasp onto.

Without knowing it, I have been keeping Solomon in a box. His name means "peace," and maybe I wanted his book to fit into certain peaceful dreams I had about things. He is described as the wisest man in the world, and maybe I wanted his book to glorify wisdom, as he does in Proverbs.

I used to enjoy reading lovers of wisdom like Plato and Aristotle, the philosophers. They wrote beautifully about how to find happiness. Their books were like a dream, full of sweet words and pleasant assurances; and perhaps that is what I wanted Ecclesiastes to be. But that is not what it is at all.

Looking back, I suppose I might also have been defensive about the church, or perhaps guilty of the presumption of thinking it needed me to save it, like Uzzah. It may have been this vanity that prevented me from allowing poor old Solomon to be himself or say what he wanted to say.

The way to make a church look good is to make it look successful. Build a massive cathedral, have a megachurch and a choir, do exciting programs, wow everyone with your preaching, present a smiling face to the world, etc. But Solomon has something simple to say about that. All is vanity.

And he was the expert. He built the most famous church of all.

The problem is the naked God on the cross. You cannot be naked and also be successful in the world. On the cross, Christ appeared to be a miserable failure. Even his own disciples deserted him. We tend to gloss over this uncomfortable fact on our way to making things shiny and nice.

It occurs to me that I haven't been looking at Christ at all, up there on his crucifix. I've been nodding at him all my life without realizing he was naked. Because I did not see he was naked, I also did not see how much he was suffering. I thought it was about the nails, but that was only physical.

He had a much deeper pain, which was his shame. He was hung up naked for all the world to see. "He that is hanged is accursed by God." His enemies laughed at him and triumphed over him. Apparently his notion of success was not their notion of success.

We talk in the church about standing at the foot of the cross, but maybe we should try looking at it from his point of view, hanging up there naked. Maybe we should think less about ourselves and where we happen to be standing and try to comprehend his deep shame.

Why? Because we are all headed to the same place. There is "one event" in which we are all naked, whether or not we want to admit it. Solomon found himself approaching this event and saw his nakedness very clearly. That's what his little book is all about.

The people standing at the foot of the cross saw their stories falling apart before their very eyes. The one they called "lord" now seemed powerless and frankly ridiculous. Until then, they had very different notions about him. They thought of him as a conqueror in the style of Joshua or David.

To see Christ on the cross was to be deprived of a story that was the source of identity and pride. It was to enter into a state of being where nothing seems real, nothing seems solid. They were lost as they stood there looking up at him, but by looking up they were also found. This is a great mystery.

The Great Reduction

Nakedness became a source of shame in the garden because of sin, and nakedness is what we see in Solomon in Ecclesiastes. He may have been "arrayed in all his glory," but in his old age he was utterly naked in another way, utterly powerless and ashamed of his weakness in one vital area.

And that is in the little matter of contentment. To see Solomon in his own words is to see a very unhappy man with no remedy in sight because he is old and has nowhere left to hide. This was doubly painful because he had cultivated the image of a wise man who knew how to make himself happy.

To the world, "wisdom" has a smiling face. It indicates that happiness has been found. But in Ecclesiastes wisdom has become a source of sorrow and vexation. Solomon is beginning to realize that wisdom is far off and cannot give him the peace he is so desperately seeking.

Aristotle wrote a charming book called the *Nicomachean Ethics*. It meanders along in its discursive way almost as if he were chatting to us in person. This discursiveness not only draws us into his argument but is also meant to represent his happiness, his contentment.

It would not be an exaggeration to say that Aristotle cast a spell over the world. Whole ages of philosophy and even theology can be traced to his sunny influence. The spell consists of his unparalleled ability to convince us that happiness is a real thing—and he has found it.

This *spell* is just what we mean by "narrative." Happiness is a cheerful tale cleverly told, and we are all under its spell. We do not have to read Aristotle to absorb it. The tale comes to us in innumerable ways, even in the underwear ad we see while watching football on dusky November afternoons.

The *Nicomachean Ethics* appears to be a book of philosophy when in fact it could also be called a very charming story. Happiness is the pretty girl, and we are all in love with her and caught up in pursuit of her. The ending of the story is a satisfactory one. Happiness has been found.

But happiness is the very thing Solomon cannot find as he tosses and turns on his bed on dark nights. A young man may be proud of his good looks, but old age takes them away. A young man may be proud of his energy and industriousness, but the time will come when he will have to lay them both aside.

The pursuit of happiness is based on some desirable goal. The reason we keep our lawn perfect and our house clean is that those things seem desirable to us, or "good." The reason we build a deck is we want to sit on it with our friends. The reason we aspire to promotion is we want more honor and money.

These things are desired not just for their own sake but for their presumed power to make us happy. They are part of what we are calling the narrative of happiness. But they are not happiness itself. We can find pleasure in them, to be sure, but not contentment; certainly not the peace we are seeking.

A guy sets out to put an addition on his house because he thinks his family needs more space and he wants to enhance the value of his property. He works hard on it, either building it himself or paying for it to be built. It seems good to him, desirable; otherwise he would not sacrifice so much.

But the addition cannot make him happy. If he built it himself, and it came out well, he can take a craftsman's pleasure in it, but even this is limited. The craftsman's highest pleasure is in crafting, which is linked to identity; he cannot enjoy the thing he made as much as the thing he is making.

He discovers that pleasure is not happiness. It is quite possible to find pleasure in the work his hands have done and still feel miserable and restless inside. And the pleasure he can receive from his work fades over the years with inevitable decay. His addition becomes subtraction.

Perhaps he feels compelled to continue to pursue the mirage of happiness with something new. But this new thing—even if it is the greatest addition in the world—will not make him happy either. It will not give him what he desires most, as Solomon found out.

The reason is *identity*, which is at the root of the pursuit of happiness in all its forms. There are many things we love, but what we love the most is our identity (generally speaking). This love is the hidden spring of all the ambitious things we might do in pursuit of some presumed good.

Either we are living for pleasure—as some claim to do—and they are not happy either—or we are trying to build something, do something, make something, achieve something. All of that doing is nothing more than the surface of something that remains unseen but is real just the same.

"All people are like the grass." Their lives are a momentary flowering in the vast continuum of time. This is the very thing that drives them to succeed. They want to do something and become someone before departing from this spinning orb, and a nagging little voice keeps driving them on.

But the same voice that drives them on will also never let them be content. Why did Beethoven write nine symphonies? Wasn't the *Eroica* enough, that astonishing masterpiece? No, it most certainly was not enough; not if you're Beethoven. It can never be enough.

Solomon is not a moralist. In fact the amazing thing about Ecclesiastes is it has no moral. Perhaps this is why it can seem unsettling to Christians. We want a moral because it implies closure. Incidentally, it also intimates winners and losers, and is therefore linked to identity.

Don't bother looking for closure in this great book, however. It is certainly not immoral—far from it—but neither does it satisfy our desire to have things wrapped up in a neat little package. It is the raw data of existence as seen through the eyes of a man who is too old to dissemble.

We used to call literature of this type a "complaint." It was not unique to Solomon. Here is his father: "My heart was hot within me, while I was musing the fire burned: then I spoke with my tongue, Lord, make me to know my end, and the measure of my days, what it is: that I may know how frail I am."

Solomon looks back on his youth and his successes and realizes that "all is vanity." He spent his life chasing after happiness only to discover in old age that he had not found it; that it was like chasing after wind. And then there was only one thing left for him, only one thing of which he was certain.

But that is the end of the story . . .

The Great Reduction

Vanity, vanity, all is vanity

When we are young, we might be inclined to read these words as a blistering critique of society and manners, like Thackeray's famous book. But that is not what they are at all. They are an outburst from an old man who has grown tired of life—and mostly of himself.

Solomon had suddenly become aware of his mortality. We'll get into this in more depth later on. Now of course we do know we are mortal, even from a young age. But in old age it ceases to be just head knowledge and becomes personal—in fact every time we look in the mirror.

This momentous shift in our point of view changes everything. Once you've seen your mortality, you cannot go back. You can't become young and careless again. You are stuck where you are. And the place where Solomon was stuck was not good.

Before going on, let us take a moment to praise happy old men. We see them all the time in movies and on TV and at the country club. We have no intention of questioning their happiness. In fact we are very glad for them—if they are happy.

But that was not what Solomon was. He was more like the rest of us. The unhappiness we experience as young men and women starts to become a little desperate as it spills over into old age, because we begin to realize that it is unlikely to go away.

We live our whole lives dreaming of the time when we will grow old and wise and retire and *be happy*. We live in hope of enjoying our "golden years." But what happens to hope when that time comes and we still are not happy? What happens when old age seems more like a trap than a release?

When we are young, we think of gray hair as a sign of contentment and being reconciled to the world. But to the person who actually has gray hair, it is a sign of old age, decline, and benign neglect. It is a sign that time is growing short, which makes unhappiness seem more pronounced.

Solomon has seen all this, and his reaction is a bitter outburst. "All is vanity." He does not mean there is nothing of value in God's creation. He does not mean there is no value in mortals or their work. He means he is still unhappy after all these years, and therefore all of his striving was in vain.

The Great Reduction

What does a man gain by all the toil with which he toils under the sun?

Staring death in the face, Solomon now realizes that it does not matter how much you build or how much you achieve or accumulate. You have to leave all that behind at the door to the grave.

He appears not to have been thinking about this until now. He wrote a glorious book that was all about obtaining prosperity and contentment through wisdom (Proverbs). What changed? He did. His perspective changed as he grew old and his youthful energy ebbed away.

There is one thing no one can gain by his toil, which is life. We can accumulate stuff and honors, but we cannot be happy with them because they cannot save us from the grave. And this suggests that life—not stuff or honors—is the thing we really want the most.

So why do we chase after the stuff and honors? Because unconsciously we think they will give us life. Our desire for life is the hidden force in all ambition and striving, hidden even from ourselves. But in old age, this desire is unveiled, and then we see the futility of our toil.

This is the analysis of our continuing unhappiness put forth by Ecclesiastes. You can decide for yourself whether it fits the facts. If so, then you may find some interesting information about contentment in this bracing old book.

The Great Reduction

A generation goes, and a generation comes,
but the earth remains forever.

A great irreducible truth has been revealed to Solomon in his old age—or through old age—and will not let him go. Any thought of the importance and uniqueness of our toil is lost when we realize that generations come and generations go.

It is hard to say exactly when this happens. Maybe it's the first time you find yourself being extra careful on the stairs or stymied by blurred words on the page. Maybe it's when the hearing starts to go. Maybe it's when you realize that the people in the nursing home are not that much older than you.

But it does happen, except in the oblivious. At some point it will become evident to all that we are far from being immortal. Our heroic struggles and toils do not make us like God. We will pass away into oblivion, and those struggles and toils will be forgotten.

For Solomon, the undertow of this realization came from the fact that it caught him while he was still unhappy. He had been toiling all his life for happiness but had not found it, and now he is beginning to realize that happiness might not be possible at all.

The Great Reduction

The sun also rises, and the sun goes down.

. . . and Solomon is still unhappy. Not only is the sun not his own personal source of life and identity, but it is also indifferent to his unhappiness and changing moods. This makes the rising and the setting of the sun wearisome to him.

It wasn't always this way. When we are young, we tend to think the sun rises and sets on us alone. It seems personal. But in fact the sun rises and sets to sustain all life on earth, not only ours. The larger context of this sorrowful reflection, then, is life.

The sun's indifference to his suffering is painful to Solomon and the shining identity he has been pursuing all his life. Instead of bringing him the dawn of a new day and a new hope, the cycles of the sun begin to mark his discontent with relentless precision.

A sunny day without joy can seem very long indeed. Solomon is looking for the restoration of the joy he once knew. He will find it, but he has a long, long way to go.

The Great Reduction

The wind returns again according to his circuits.

That is, according to God's inscrutable plan. Like the sun, the wind is indifferent to us and our little struggles. The plan for the wind is not known to us and has nothing to do with our hopes for happiness. It has a purpose, a function in the natural order of things, but it is not to our purposes.

The reason this thought is oppressive to Solomon is it shows him his nothingness. The winds do not change when Solomon is unhappy; they do not adjust themselves to give him good cheer. The more he understands about the winds, the more his sense of nothingness and dislocation increases.

The wisdom he has obtained about the winds only increases his sorrow. And in fact the sorrows of wisdom will become an important theme as we go along—which is all the more amazing when we consider that Solomon sought identity in wisdom.

The Great Reduction

The rivers run into the sea, and yet the sea is never full.

This could be Solomon's motto. Think of the sea as identity. All the rivers of his highly productive life ran into this thirsty sea, but it can never be filled because he could never give himself the one thing he really wanted, the only thing that could make him happy.

And this one thing is life. The desire for an enduring identity is the engine of all our striving, and it is rooted in the desire for life. We don't want fame for its own sake; we want fame because we want our identity to live. This shows that our highest value is life.

The Bible is unique in linking happiness to the desire for life. Adam and Eve were in paradise as long as they had access to the tree of life; their misery commenced when they were cut off permanently from that tree. That's a poetic way of saying only life can make us happy.

"The people living in darkness have seen a great light." But what is this light? It is the resurrected life. Christ is glorified specifically because he obtained life. "In him was life, and this life was the light of the world." John links the happiness that is found in him directly to life.

Today we have another tree that gives us access to life. But Solomon knew nothing of this tree. He was among the people living in darkness. All his life he tried to obtain happiness by being a superstar. What he was actually trying to obtain, without knowing it, was life.

All the rivers of his ambition flowed into this sea, but it was never full. There was no rest for him, no respite from his labors, because it was not possible to obtain the happiness of life. And now he is beginning to see the futility of all his striving.

We are told there is a river that can satisfy eternal longings, the same river that "makes glad the city of God." Ezekiel saw it, and it was last seen flowing down the streets of the new Jerusalem, quickening everything it touches, turning brown branches into life.

This river can fill the sea of our longing because it represents the Spirit, who is the Lord and giver of life. But the age of the Spirit had not yet come. All Solomon could see from his disadvantaged viewpoint was the futility and weariness of striving to make himself happy.

The Great Reduction

Unto the place from whence the rivers come, there they return again.

Solomon's great soul-weariness is marked by the theme of the perpetual return, which he will bring up repeatedly.

We will ask your permission, dear reader, to use this term without invoking Nietzsche or Buddhism or the "eternal return," the reincarnation meme, which is a very different thing.

Aristotle tells us all good stories have a beginning, a middle, and an ending. That's because all good stories are rooted in identity. They have an ending because identity requires closure in order to be happy. The ending sets the story and the identity it provides apart from other stories.

But Solomon has seen something terrifying: the rivers return from whence they came. God's artfulness in providing for our needs—the cycles through which evaporation of the seas brings us clouds and rain and rivers return to the sea—has become oppressive to him by taking away happy endings.

The rivers are *always* returning to themselves. And the same is true of the rivers of striving that we pour into the sea of unfulfilled desire. The moment we see them returning, the ending of the story is undone, and it is no longer possible for our endeavors to make us happy.

It now occurs to Solomon that the stories he has been telling himself do not have a happy ending. He thought he was accomplishing something when he was participating in the perpetual return. Nature never grows weary in her cycles, but this is not the case with old men, as he is about to tell us.

The Great Reduction

All things are full of labor; man cannot utter it.

The rivers are always flowing into the sea. The seasons are always changing. The bird is always feathering its nest or looking for something to eat. The squirrel is always storing up nuts. The tides come and go with the phases of the moon.

When you are young, this perpetual exchange of energy is energizing; but when you are old it may seem exhausting and pointless. Solomon looks upon all the ceaseless labor of nature and is appalled. There is no rest. There is no peace.

The world too is full of labor. The most ambitious among us are constantly toiling. It was not enough for Solomon to build the temple; he had to build a palace too. It was not enough for him to write an exquisitely beautiful love song, the greatest ever penned; he had to write a thousand.

But we are not like nature's creatures. We grow old and long for rest. We have a home that is not our natural home. We are looking for a place that is not the place where we live and have our being, and this is the source of our discontent.

The Great Reduction

The eye is not satisfied with seeing, nor the ear filled with hearing.

We can see or hear beautiful things and enjoy them, but the eye and ear always want more. This is the law of desire. Or as Solomon says in Proverbs, "Hell and destruction are never full; so the eyes of man are never satisfied."

When we are young, desire seems like a blessing. Let the seeing and the hearing commence! And when we say "young," we think this feeling probably extends well into middle age, while the life-spirit remains strong and we have not become too reflective.

But a strange thing has happened to Solomon, who is now well beyond middle age. As former pleasures fade, he has seen the dark side of desire. The eye is *never* satisfied; the ear is *never* filled. And this poses a problem for someone who longs for contentment.

To be content is to be *filled*. Desire ceases its restless striving because we already have what we want. But then contentment and the desires of the ears and eyes are at odds with each other. The eyes and ears continue to seek pleasure but can never be satisfied.

Solomon is speaking philosophically. The pleasures of nature, for example, as great as they are—and they are incomparable—cannot provide contentment. The very force that makes them seem so desirable also deprives us of the rest we are seeking.

The fault is not in them but in ourselves. They cannot fill us because we have another longing that we are trying to satisfy with the things of this world. And this is even more true of the things we ourselves have made or won or earned.

Solomon built a famous temple, but his eyes could not be satisfied with it. He heaped up gold, but it did not make him happy. He married seven hundred wives, but he longed for a single wife whom he could love and who would sincerely love him in return.

The eye is never satisfied because the soul desires life. Thus the great pleasures of the eyes can become a curse as well as a blessing.

The Great Reduction

The thing that has been is that which shall be.

More on the theme of the perpetual return.

Old people are tired. They do not have rest from the pleasures of seeing and hearing, but they may be tired of those pleasures. They do not have rest from their labors, the rest they were seeking all along, but they are tired of their labors and cannot go on.

This puts them in a strange predicament. They continue to be restless, but their weariness now stands in the way of contentment. The only way to make this clear is to make their weariness clear; which is just what Solomon is going to do, at some length.

First, the thing that has been is what shall be. Or as he will say later, there is nothing new under the sun. You are blissfully unaware of this when you are young because, well, you are young. You have not lived long enough to see the perpetual return.

The passion of the moment is what governs youth. We think we are Changing Things, and this energizes our labors. But the older we get, the more conscious we become that things never really change. Yesterday's big initiative is replaced with tomorrow's big initiative—and in that sense they are the same.

Think of the professional baseball team. There are certain things they must do in order to win the World Series. But once they have won one, those things do not change. They still have to do them in order to win. And twenty years later they have to do them all over again.

Or think of the brave young DA who has come to town to clean up things and put an end to corruption. If she is a very energetic young woman, she may succeed in cleaning up some things, but she will never put an end to corruption. There will be many DAs after her following the same path to glory.

This is the perpetual return. While we are engaged in our labors we do not see their repetitive nature. We think we are accomplishing something great, something new. But when we grow a little older and see other people doing the same things, we realize that history has a repetitive quality.

The Great Reduction

The thing is done over and over again and nothing really changes. Success does not give us what we are looking for. It does not bring happiness or closure. This is why the thing itself—the effort, the great initiative—has become wearisome to Solomon in his old age.

The Great Reduction

Is there anything of which it might be said, See, this is new?

Not really, no. Oh sure, there are new *things*, like computers and jets; but Solomon was not thinking of exterior things. He was thinking about the arcs of our lives.

Aren't we all children at one time who go to school? Don't we all grow up and get married and have children of our own and jobs we think are important? Aren't we all interested in making our homes comfy? Don't we all have our favorite sports teams and political parties?

Is there anything new in all this? We can hear Rosalind speaking as clearly to us today as the bright young girl who lives next door. We can empathize with Diomedes when he says the war he fought with such great success did not lead to the happiness he was seeking.

Their old stories are just like our stories because, no, there is nothing really new. There is only the perpetual return and the sense of weariness it can produce in the soul.

The Great Reduction

There is no remembrance of former things.

Aha—we caught him. Of course we remember former things! There are histories. There are whole museums.

But that is not what Solomon has in mind. First, histories are seventy-eight percent stories. We are not remembering the past so much as we are seeing someone's interpretation of the past.

Solomon knew about Job and Abraham and Moses and Joshua and some of the things they had done. Very few people make it into written histories, however. And in the case of the vast majority of us it is literally true that there is no remembrance of former things.

If you don't think so, try to find out the history of your own town. Try to find out what was going on in the life of the average citizen, your counterpart, two hundred years ago. You can't. It is literally as if the vast majority of those who lived in the past had never even existed.

Consider the case of Sally Barnes, resident of the bucolic town of Sherman, Connecticut, from 1771 to 1846. Sally was once very likely a fresh-faced young highland lass, full of dreams. She may have been a great mother and neighbor; she certainly has a prime view. But who remembers her now?

More, outside of her little circle of family and friends, who even knew that she existed in her own time? Did they know about Sally in the lively town of Danbury, just twenty miles south, or in the blooming metropolis of New York, a little further down the road?

Here's an interesting exercise: How many of us know the names of our own great-grandparents? If we do not know them, then how can we expect anyone else to know them? And if no one knows them, then isn't Solomon simply speaking the truth when he says there is no remembrance of former things?

The Great Reduction

I the Preacher was king over Israel in Jerusalem.

Here he identifies himself as Solomon. Some wags would say "with" Solomon. Either way, the meaning is the same. The unhappiness this man is experiencing is all the more remarkable because he is the king, and everyone expects kings to be happy.

Or at the very least, they expect them to hide any unhappiness they might have. Ecclesiastes is like David going up into his chambers to weep after Absalom was slain. Sorrow and unhappiness are signs of weakness in a king. The nation and its captains would prefer they not be seen.

Solomon's name is ironic. It means peace, which in one sense is appropriate since he reigned over Israel in a time of peace; but he himself is not at peace. Far from it. He who brought peace to Israel is troubled in his soul, almost beyond his ability to express it.

So then there are two kinds of peace. There is exterior peace where all is outwardly placid, calm; and then there is inner peace, shalom, the "peace that passes all understanding." Solomon had the first but not the second. But of what value is the first without the second?

Solomon is the king, and his name means peace, but he is not the king of peace. The purpose of Ecclesiastes is to make this abundantly clear.

The Great Reduction

And I gave my heart to seek and search out by wisdom concerning all things that are done under heaven.

Now of course we all know that when God offered to give Solomon his heart's desire, the one thing he asked for was wisdom, specifically to rule and judge the nation of Israel at a tender age. This indicated that he loved wisdom; he desired it more than any other thing.

Here he says he "gave his heart" to it. He had an inquisitive mind, like Marcus Aurelius or Thomas Jefferson. He had a passion to know about "all things that are done under heaven." He was curious about nature and how it works, and also about human nature, and the nature of being.

This makes Solomon a very unique king. Plato talks about the philosopher-king, but it does not seem to have been a common type throughout history. Solomon was also a philosopher of the best kind. He understood the true point of philosophy, which is to find the supreme good of happiness.

He wrote a book about it. The purpose of Proverbs was to show us how to make life happy by following the light of Wisdom. It is a completely practical book. There is no hint of academicism or of trying to impress others with one's capacity for abstract reasoning.

And every word in it is true. All the advice Solomon gives is very good advice. He depicts Wisdom as a woman standing on the street corner and calling out to humanity to come and eat that which is wholesome and sweet, that which can satisfy. Wisdom, in this view, is the key to contentment.

Proverbs is also a deep book. Solomon informs us that "a soft answer turns away wrath" and a "gentle tongue can break a bone." These observations are true, but they are by no means self-evident. They go against all instinctive wisdom and human nature itself.

Through his proverbs and judgments, Solomon earned a reputation as the wisest man in the world. The Queen of Sheba, laden with riches, came to riddle him because of this shimmering reputation. But this raises a very interesting question.

How is it possible that the wisest man in the world could wind up being so very unhappy?

The Great Reduction

A sore travail to fatigue themselves with.

At one time there was nothing he wanted more than to pursue wisdom, but in his old age he has come to regard it as a *sore travail* that eventually brings great weariness.

Don't worry; he is going to tell us why later on. But for the moment let's think about the change itself. It is a simple fact that we all grow weary as we grow old. Projects we would not have hesitated to undertake begin to seem daunting if not impossible.

Part of this is the loss of energy and strength. But partly it is something else, too. Our perspective on the ambitious projects of youth changes. We no longer see them in a glowing light. Knowing they cannot make us happy, we begin to have doubts about their value.

The project Solomon has in mind is his avid pursuit of wisdom. Just as it is possible to become skeptical about the excellent addition which we have built with our own hands, so it is possible to become skeptical about the pursuit of wisdom if it does not lead to happiness.

There is no identity more desirable than that of a wise man or woman. You can be a successful politician or a great athlete or musician, but if you do not have wisdom you are a very inferior star. Everyone admires wisdom. Everyone loves wisdom because to have it is to know how to be happy.

But in Solomon's case—not so much. Wisdom, the thing he used to love with all his heart, now seems like a great travail to him, hard to obtain, and, as we will see, sometimes even harder to bear.

The Great Reduction

I have seen all the works that are done under the sun;
and behold, all is vanity and vexation of spirit.

Why has wisdom become a burden? Partly because it reveals things like this to him.

All of our great works are vanity because we do them for identity. When we are building our addition with our own hands we are also building ourselves. The addition is an outward thing of finite value, but the labor and devotion are inward and full of dreaming.

It is the disparity between the dream and reality that becomes exposed over time. We begin to realize we did not build the addition just to expand our living space but also to expand ourselves. And when happiness does not materialize we begin to wonder if it was an exercise in vanity.

Our spirit is vexed because we did not obtain what we were looking for. We wanted happiness but what we found was sore travail and a certain emptiness. All works done under the sun are scorched by the sun. They cannot give us the refreshment we desire.

Other than his writings, the "work" for which Solomon was most famous was the temple he built. No, he did not build it with his own hands, but it was his firm hand that carried it through to completion. Surely such a magnificent accomplishment can make a man happy!

But this was not the case. No edifice, no matter how splendid, can fill up the infinite space of our longing. As soon as it is built we begin to have doubts about it. We see things that could have been done better. We wonder how we could have been so stupid as to miss them.

Worse, nothing in this world is permanent. The temple cannot give Solomon the identity he desires because it will not last forever. He was explicitly warned that it would not last if Israel did not remain faithful. And in a time of great unfaithfulness it was utterly destroyed.

Solomon had an example of the futility of great works right next door in the pyramids. The Egyptians, thinking their kings were divine and lived on after death, filled the pyramids with things the kings would need in the afterlife. Those things remained untouched until the tomb raiders came along.

Our works, no matter how great they may be, become vexing when we see that they cannot fill the sea of our desire. They cannot make us happy. We must look somewhere else.

The Great Reduction

That which is crooked cannot be made straight.

Through our great works and search for wisdom we are trying to redress a certain perceived crookedness. We want to present an upright image to the world—we want to be straight—but we cannot deceive ourselves. In old age it becomes very plain that what is crooked cannot be made straight.

Solomon has had his own crookedness revealed to him. For one thing, he debased marriage with his multiple wives and concubines. He had a personal warning about taking foreign wives and turning away to their gods, and yet he did it anyway.

There was also a warning in the law. While the Israelites were still wandering in the desert, they were told that if they appoint a king, "neither shall he multiply wives to himself, that his heart turn not away: neither shall he greatly multiply to himself silver and gold."

Solomon did both of those things to glorious excess, as he himself tells us. The purpose of Proverbs was to make the crooked straight, but in his old age Solomon has seen that what is crooked cannot be made straight, not by human hands anyway. The crookedness is part of who we are.

Augustine had a term for this, but we will not use it here. Suffice it to say that old men know their crookedness better than anyone, lying awake on their beds under the cold, full moon. But to someone like Solomon, this is a crushing revelation. What good is his wisdom if he cannot make the crooked straight?

In fact, it is no good. The only way we can ever be truly happy is to have an identity that is straight, that reflects our heroic concept of ourselves, our desire to be thought of as good. This is the identity the philosophers tried to obtain through their endless discussions about "the good."

But if we are crooked by nature, then wisdom is powerless to give us what we want. We can be the wisest man in the world, like Solomon, but our wisdom cannot make us straight. This is the reason for Solomon's reevaluation of wisdom, the thing he loved the most.

The Great Reduction

That which is wanting cannot be numbered.

Another take on the same idea. It is literally impossible to number that which is wanting.

We have theories or accountings of government laid down over the ages by the wisest sages, but no one has ever counted up the perfect government. Much of the time it is not even clear to us what is holding the world together, other than sheer inertia.

We have seen many marvelous medical advances, but we cannot take away crippling arthritis; we cannot cure cancer; if someone has "essential hypertension" we cannot make it unessential; if someone has tinnitus, we cannot make his ears stop ringing.

The more minute our measurements become, the more we see that no amount of labor will ever amount to a full accounting. The human body alone is so complex with its complementary systems and redundancies that literally hundreds of peer-reviewed journals are dedicated to trying to understand it.

The stars in the sky—who has counted them? Or the molecules in a fingernail? Who has counted up weather systems and fully understands them? We can see the effects, but the causes remain hidden from our eyes. The best we can do is to jump in at some vantage point and try to defend our hypothesis.

And alas, our own behavior cannot be counted. We think and say one thing but do another. Paul has a brilliant description of this in Romans. We can love what is good, and will to do what is good, but we still wind up doing the very thing we resolved not to do.

Most of all, what is lacking in us is life. This difference cannot be counted. The philosopher cannot overcome the difference between life and mortal life through the full accounting of his wisdom. But then his wisdom cannot give him the thing he desires most.

Just how wise is the wisest man in the world if what is lacking cannot be counted? If he lacks happiness, how can he count himself happy? Solomon is beginning to see that wisdom has its limits. And this is personal for him, because he sought his identity in wisdom.

The Great Reduction

Solomon made it his life's ambition to become wise by counting what is lacking. Now he is beginning to entertain the possibility that what is lacking cannot be counted.

The Great Reduction

> *Behold, I have come to greatness,*
> *and have more wisdom than all who went before me in Jerusalem.*

No, this is not a boast. It is a lament. He became the wisest man in the world, and one of its greatest, but now he finds that neither his wisdom nor his greatness can give him peace.

He thought he was filling up a hole with wisdom and greatness, but he was creating a bigger one. Why? Because "all men are like the grass." If it is life we want, which is our own built-in standard of greatness, then wisdom cannot give us what we are looking for.

All wisdom can do is show us that we have fallen short of the mark.

The Great Reduction

I gave myself to know wisdom and madness and folly,
and I perceived that this too is vexation of spirit.

"Madness and folly" mean, we think, that which is contrary to reason. If someone knows that provoking his neighbor leads to great grief, and yet continues to do it, then this is "madness" in the sense that he is not listening to his own rational faculties.

Solomon wanted to know madness and folly as contrarieties to wisdom. He wanted to know what wisdom is through its difference from that which is madness and folly. But as we know, there was a bit of a glitch in this plan. Solomon himself was no stranger to folly.

For example, he was not wise enough to avoid worshiping his wives' foreign gods. What could be more foolish than worshiping things we make with our own hands, as the prophets said? What could be more mad than to ignore what God has done for us and turn away from his everlasting love?

And yet this is just what Solomon did. It is a vexing thing to learn, as we grow older, that the madness and folly we decry in others are also seen in ourselves. In old age, wisdom and madness and folly fall into a foolish embrace.

The Great Reduction

> *For in much wisdom is much grief,*
> *and he that increases knowledge increases sorrow.*

This is the exact opposite of what the philosophers tell us, by the way. They want us to believe that wisdom and knowledge are the key to obtaining the good of happiness. Solomon believed this himself at one time. He does not believe it anymore.

When you are twenty-five, it is easy to convince yourself that you can obtain happiness through the pursuit of wisdom at, say, twenty-six. It becomes much harder to believe this when you are sixty-five. Wisdom and knowledge become vexatious when they cannot give you what you long for.

You have obtained a reputation as the wisest man in the world, and still you are not at peace. How then has your love of wisdom helped you? The Queen of Sheba loves you for your wisdom. This is flattering, but if you are unhappy then how much have you really gained?

The Great Reduction

*I said in my heart, go to; now I will prove you with mirth;
therefore enjoy pleasure.*

A pox on your artificial chapter breaking, Archbishop Langton! In this case it leads to a very misleading conclusion.

Turning to pleasure in his search for happiness is the direct result of what has gone before. Solomon is describing his own life. Embittered by his pursuit of wisdom, which did not bring him happiness, he decided in his frustration to seek happiness in pleasure.

We have seen comparisons to Epicurus, but pleasure was Epicurus's *first* choice, not his last resort. Pleasure was first for Epicurus because, in his view, God did not make the world and had no connection to the affairs of men. This would have meant nothing to Solomon.

Epicurus tried to obtain tranquility of mind by using pleasure to blot out any thought of God and death. The exact opposite is seen in Solomon. God is the source of simple pleasures like work and food and drink, and enjoying them is a way to enjoy the goodness of God.

This idea is found throughout the Old Testament. "For you, Lord, have made me glad through your work: I will triumph in the works of your hands." God made all things good, and therefore to find pleasure in them is to rejoice in the goodness of God. Epicurus believed no such thing.

Now in one sense it is indisputably true that God's creation gives great pleasure; for instance, the flavor of honey, or the beauty and fragrance of a rose, or the morning light. Such things are "very good," highly pleasurable. Epicurus's contention that they somehow obtained their goodness randomly by natural processes is a hypothesis that cannot be proven by the empiricism he himself recommends.

Yes, much pleasure can be found in the pleasurable things God has made; but, contrary to Epicurus, those things cannot make us happy. And the reason, as Solomon is about to inform us, is that God has put eternity into our hearts. This makes it impossible to obtain the tranquility of mind we long for by attempting, through pleasure, to put aside any thought of death.

The Great Reduction

Solomon's experiments with pleasure were disappointing. He tried laughter and found it to be madness. Laughter can be salutary when it is spontaneous, but this becomes rarer with age. Mirth—what does it accomplish? Why do we want to seem mirthful? Because we want others to think we are happy? This show of mirth cannot actually *make* us happy.

It cannot make us the thing we are pretending to be. Once we have seen ourselves laughing, laughter can never mean the same thing to us again. Solomon tried laughter as a solution to his unhappiness, but laughter cannot be *tried*. Forced laughter is mirthless mirth and joyless pleasure.

What about wine? It makes us feel happy through intoxication, but too much wine leads to loss of self-control and a bad ending. Solomon undertakes his assay of wine "yet acquainting my heart with wisdom"—that is, trying to find the golden mean of wine.

This golden mean is real. He who would indulge in wine is well-advised to follow it. Moderation in wine, as in all things, is the best way. A little wine in company is convivial; too much can lead to bitterness that lingers for a long time.

Since sober wisdom did not make Solomon happy, he decided to try the seeming folly of wine. Revelry seems like folly to many who are in love with philosophy, but what if it is tried in a philosophical manner, not for its own sake, but experimentally, to see what is good for humankind?

What if wine-induced "folly" is tried as the antidote to the grief found in wisdom? Solomon tried it, but it did not make him happy. If wine could give true happiness, Epicurus would be the world's greatest philosopher. There would be no thought of anyone else.

The brain is a strange thing. It tells us to move by having an inhibitory neurotransmitter turn down the inhibitory effects of the internal pallidus on the thalamus. That is, it disinhibits by inhibiting inhibition. The same is true of alcohol. The immediate effect is euphoria; the net effect is dysphoria.

Solomon tried the mirthfulness of wine in an attempt to take away the sorrows of his pursuit of wisdom—we will come to that in just a moment—and discovered it was folly in the sense that it did not give him the happiness he desired.

Solomon is a true philosopher when so many others are fabricators and storytellers. He posits a means to happiness; he tries it; and then he honestly reports on the results.

The Great Reduction

I made me great works.

Why "great"? Because Solomon was looking for greatness in his works. And his works were indeed great—but the identity he was seeking continued to elude him.

For one thing, great works cannot make anyone good. We have plenty of examples of people who made great works but were neither great nor good, who lived selfishly and treated others badly and sucked all the oxygen out of the room.

Therefore it does not follow that great works make great men. It makes men who may appear to the world to be great, but that is a different thing entirely. They know their own lack of goodness; therefore greatness cannot make them happy.

Solomon was a nonpareil maker of great works. "I built me houses" is the understatement of all time. We have a clear record of the great houses he built; not only his palace but the incomparable temple, described in loving detail.

But the temple he built cannot make him great. It can make him great in *our* minds, perhaps, but not in his own. Solomon knew he was not good and will say so in a moment. Otherwise he would not have been so unhappy. The greatness he obtained through great works was an illusion.

Nor is any great work permanent. Future generations would not see the great things Solomon made. It takes a shallow man to find contentment in the greatness of fleeting things. This is why it was possible for Solomon to make great works and still be unhappy.

One of our famous actors commented that he wished everyone could obtain fame so they could see how completely empty and meaningless it is. Greatness in the world is greatly desired, but it cannot give us peace. All it does is reveal the extent of our emptiness.

Solomon made orchards and gardens and reservoirs to water them. But great gardens must be maintained with great effort. Who will love his gardens the way he did after he is gone? Is it not just as likely that they will plow them over and plant some grass, with sheep to mow it?

Would they be any less wise than Solomon if they did; that is, less content?

The Great Reduction

*I got myself servants and maidens,
and many servants were born in my house.*

Well, of course you did! We all love to be served, and in the ancient world we added to our collective wealth and importance by allowing servants to multiply. And don't be so modest; you also enslaved the neighboring peoples when needed for your massive building projects.

Now before we subject poor Solomon to Howard Zinn treatment on the question of slavery, please recall that slavery was a universal condition of existence in the ancient world. Nor was it necessarily chattel slavery. Poor men sold themselves or their children into slavery to get out of debt, and those born to slavery often had little incentive to break free.

Slavery was universal in those times because household chores and tasks that we take for granted used to require hours of massive labor. Those who had the means acquired servants to do the things they did not have the time or energy to do themselves.

Slavery also became important to Solomon because of his building projects—like the temple, the palace, the wall around Jerusalem. In this Solomon followed the custom of the ancient world. Great building projects generally required slave or forced labor because everything had to be done by hand.

And yet multiplication of servants is multiplication of sorrows. First, it is a moral burden. It is wrong for some men to own others and force them to work without fair wages. There is little joy in such ownership for the lover of wisdom when it is accompanied by a pained conscience.

Second, slaves are a grave responsibility. They must be clothed and fed and cared for, just like one's own children. They are human beings. They have the same complexities as their masters; owning them is not as simple as owning horses or cows.

We may think that if we can get people to serve us, then we will have peace and leisure and be happy. But by a great irony, servitude may bring more peace to the one who serves than to the one who is being served—if he knows how to value it.

In service there might be freedom, in ownership none.

The Great Reduction

*I also possessed more cattle, great and small,
than any in Jerusalem before me.*

Interesting, isn't it, how those two ideas—possession and greatness—seem to flow so easily together? It is not just the thought that he had all those cattle that tickles his fancy; it is that he had more than anyone before him. The love of possession is about identity.

But this is precisely why our possessions cannot make us happy. We think they can, but once we obtain them we discover they do not have this magical power. As soon as our fields are filled with cattle, a new kind of restlessness appears.

Actually cattle make a good case study for the limitations of possessions. They eat a lot. They get sick and may die. With certain types of diseases, the whole herd must be culled. Perhaps we build a barn for them, to protect our wealth, but then the barn must be maintained.

Given all this, it is not difficult to see why Thoreau said our possessions wind up possessing us. They do not give us the freedom or happiness we desire. The more we have, the more they can become another form of slavery, one we impose upon ourselves.

All possessions are passing away into the land of shadows. The owner of cattle knows this better than anyone. Solomon must be very assiduous about breeding, as he apparently is with his slaves, in order to keep from losing all he possesses and his pride.

The problem for a philosopher like Solomon is that he cannot help seeing these things. He cannot be blind to the limitations of his possessions. And then the identity he was seeking in his acquisitiveness comes back to him on a string.

He got himself silver and gold! Sure he did—he took them away from the kings and the provinces and from his own people through heavy taxation. Silver and gold are not like cattle; they do not get diseases or die. Everyone acknowledges they are precious. Surely they will make him happy!

But the more we have, the more we want. The richer we are, the more our neighbors envy and despise us. Even our children may begin to secretly wish for our demise, since we are worth more to them dead than alive.

He got himself singers and musicians! Music is one of the sweetest gifts of heaven, and a king was known for the musicians he kept at court and his love of culture. But music is a fickle thing. The tune that makes us happy today may seem tedious tomorrow.

Music cannot make us happy. If it could, there would not be so many unhappy musicians in the world. And as Solomon will tell us later on, when you grow old and deaf you can no longer hear the music you are maintaining in your palace at such great expense.

The Great Reduction

*So I was great and increased more than all
who had been in Jerusalem before me.*

These valuable things are not acquired merely for their own sake. They are acquired for the sake of being "great." The hidden force in all extremes of acquisitiveness is identity. But acquiring things did not make Solomon happy, not even a court full of gold and musicians.

The things Solomon acquired may give him greatness in other people's eyes, but not in his own. Because of our nakedness, our mortal limitations, nothing we ourselves can obtain can make us feel great. As soon as we have them, we realize how inadequate they are.

This demonstrable fact discloses the existence of a desire that cannot be satisfied with things. It was never the things themselves that Solomon longed for; it was greatness. And he longed for greatness because he wanted to cover up his nakedness.

Today we cast our eyes with joy upon the golden goblet we have acquired; tomorrow we see it with diminishing joy; and the day after that we are already leaning toward indifference. How can the thing that gave us joy today not give us joy tomorrow?

What has changed? Not the goblet. It is just as beautiful and valuable as ever. No, the change is in us. Possession becomes stale when it loses the freshness to hide our nakedness.

Also my wisdom remained with me.

None of these things were done without self-awareness. Solomon did not try them slavishly, but with an eye toward wisdom. There was something he wanted to know, something he wanted to try out: Can any of these things, embellished with wisdom, give happiness?

Alas, none of them had that most-desired power. His wisdom stayed with him because he saw they could not give him what he wanted. He does us the great service of standing in for us. Few can accomplish what he accomplished; but we can come to his little book and find out the truth.

Accomplishments and possessions are *vanity* in the sense that they cannot fill the hole in our being—that is, they are done in vain. And they are vanity in another sense as well, since the desire for them is rooted in identity, a sea that can never be filled by human effort.

Dreaming about such things instead of enjoying the life we have and the things given freely from the hand of God—this is vanity.

The Great Reduction

And whatsoever my eyes desired I did not keep from them.

He denied himself *nothing* that seemed desirable to his eyes. He had the power and wealth to do this because he was the king, And still he was unhappy.

Acquisition cannot make us happy because there is no thing, no matter how precious it may seem, that can satisfy the desires of the soul, which is immortal. There can be great joy in the acquisition of the thing; but once acquired, this joy immediately begins to fade.

So then our eyes deceive us. If it were only the thing for its own sake that we desired, then it might make us happy. But our desire for valuable things is mixed up with another desire the eyes cannot see. Thus our eyes fill us with false hope.

The desire to obtain things through labor is also deceptive. There can be great joy in building that addition for ourselves, but as soon as it is done we discover something strange about human nature. It is not the thing itself that gives us joy; it is the labor with which we sought to obtain it.

We were made in the image of the creator, which makes us creative by nature. "I withheld not my heart from any joy; for my heart rejoiced in all my labor: and joy was my portion of all my labor." This is good news and bad news. His labor gave him joy, but the thing that he thought he wanted was vanity.

Our great endeavors give us joy because we think the thing we are laboring for can make us happy. But if we have been laboring to make things for the sake of happiness, and in the end those things do not make us happy, then "all is vanity."

Our efforts were in vain because they did not give us the thing we desired most. But by this reduction, something is left over—the labor itself. Solomon is heading toward a remarkable conclusion about the things that truly give peace and contentment.

The Great Reduction

> *Then I looked at all the things my hands had made,*
> *and all the labor I had labored to do, and look you now:*
> *it was vanity and vexation of spirit.*

Let's think about this for a moment in a purely practical way. The addition we labored so hard to make—thinking it would make us happy—can never reach up to our high hopes. We can be pleased with it, but it cannot give us contentment.

It seems we have a *built-in resistance* to being fully satisfied with anything we ourselves have made. Yes, even Shakespeare, even Jane Austen, even Beethoven. If anything, they were more likely to be unsatisfied than we are, because the greater the enterprise the more insurmountable the difficulties.

Call it the law of proportionate incommensurability. Sure, if you or I make an addition to our house, we can never be satisfied because we are not great artists; but what about those other worthies? What about the greatest artists and makers of things, like Solomon?

They can't be happy either. It seems we are all reaching for something beyond our grasp. You and I have one thing in common with Beethoven and Solomon: nothing we can do will ever make us happy. We think we would be happy if we could do what they did. But were they happy?

Solomon experienced a force of *resistance* to all the great buildings he had made. According to the Bible, this resistance comes from the difference between life and mortal life. We cannot be satisfied with anything we do because everything we do reveals our nakedness.

We tend to hide our discontent, but not Solomon. He comes right out and admits that the great things he accomplished did not make him happy. In fact they became a source of vexation. No matter how great they may seem to others, they can never seem that way to him.

Suppose there were two realms of reality; two "kingdoms." And suppose in one realm there was a perfection of which everything in the other realm was a copy or shadow. In that case, no matter how hard we worked on perfecting the copy, it would never make us happy.

The Great Reduction

Let's say we build our tabernacle or temple based on a pattern we are shown of perfection; indeed, on the basis of a mountaintop experience. It does not matter how careful we are—we are still dealing with a pattern. It is not the thing itself; it is merely a representation of the thing.

The pattern Moses saw on the mountain signifies the realm of life. It signifies the thing we desire most, but it is not that thing. It is a shadow of it. Solomon probably used this pattern to inform his great temple, which replaced the tabernacle, intuiting its importance from Moses's instructions.

But here's the thing. If it were possible to make ourselves happy, then the *pattern* would mean nothing to us at all. The very existence of the pattern means we cannot obtain what we are looking for. The pattern tells us the other realm is real, and the best we can do is to represent it.

Today we have a very different perspective on the pattern Moses saw. It represents not a building but the church—the body of believers. The harmony of the parts signifies the body of Christ and the unity of the Spirit through which we obtain peace and knowledge of God.

Christ builds his church by giving us life. The peace we are looking for is made possible by his sacrifice. But nothing in the *world* can give us peace. Solomon built the great temple, but his restlessness shows that it was not the real church he was seeking. It was just a pattern of that church.

The Great Reduction

And behold, Solomon was naked.

No, that's not in the book! But it is the truth. Solomon is a naked old man in Ecclesiastes, wrinkles and all. Not a pretty sight. We want to avert our eyes. The book makes us uncomfortable because he does no posing or pretending.

Solomon did the thing you do not do. Remember his father boasting on his death bed? That's the way to go out—on top. But Solomon was in no mood for boasting in old age. He was unhappy, and the wisdom he loved so much would not allow him to pretend otherwise.

He tells us he looked at all the great things he had done, and not only did they not make him happy, but they were a *vexation*. You don't say things like this in polite company. In our everyday patois everyone is happy. We want other people to think so, anyway.

"What does it profit a man to gain the whole world and lose his own soul?" We know Solomon has not lost his soul yet because he now counts all worldly gain as loss. And he is very open about it.

The Great Reduction

> *Then I turned to behold wisdom and madness and folly;*
> *for what can a man do that comes after the king?*

The king he had in mind, alas, was his father. This was personal for Solomon. His greatest accomplishment was the temple, but his father was the one who planned and provided for it. Solomon was always following in the footsteps of another.

This was the case with anything he might do. He was the son of Israel's greatest king. There was nothing Solomon could ever do to displace his father from the hearts of the people of Israel, or even to make himself equal to his father.

When he says "what can a man do," he means to obtain greatness. He has seen that there is nothing he can do that will make him as beloved as his father. This is not a random observation. It falls right in line with everything he has been saying.

He wants an identity like his father's but cannot obtain it. He cannot outdo his father, although he tried. And this simple fact reveals something important to him. "All is vanity." It is impossible to obtain the immortal identity for which Solomon is longing.

Many people have lived through his pain, sons and daughters of the famous actor, the pastor, the politician, the successful. Sometimes their lives are destroyed by the fame of the parent. Their own longing for identity is made too painful to bear because of the successes the parent has had.

Think about this from Solomon's point of view. Could he defeat the archenemies that had already been defeated, the Philistines? Could he build a city more beautiful than Jerusalem? Could he compose something more perfect or beloved than the twenty-third psalm?

Solomon turned to behold wisdom and madness and folly because he wanted to do something *different* from David. He wanted to do something to distinguish himself, to show that he too was a "great man." But he is about to reveal the limitations of this effort.

The Great Reduction

Then I saw that wisdom exceeds folly as light exceeds darkness.

Solomon, the guy who put wisdom on a pedestal, is now going to put wisdom into perspective. He takes a circuitous route, maybe because his message is almost more than he himself can bear, but it all boils down to this: wisdom is better than folly, but wisdom cannot give us peace.

Solomon begins his reevaluation of wisdom by conceding that it is decisively better than folly. The plain, practical wisdom seen in Proverbs leads to a much happier, much better life than the folly of ignoring it and not using our heads. This is incontrovertibly true.

"Go to the ant, you sluggard; consider her ways and be wise." It is quite simply true that laziness is not the path to prosperity or accomplishment. Laziness benefits no one, least of all the one who is lazy. The ant shows us that industriousness, on any scale, is constructive.

Anyone who heeds this wisdom will lead a happier life than those who do not. Ergo, wisdom is better than folly. But while wisdom can give us much happiness, it cannot make us happy. It does not matter how industrious we are; nothing can spare us from the day of reckoning.

The Great Reduction

The wise man's eyes are in his head, while the fool walks in darkness; but I also perceived that one event happens to them all.

Certainly it is better to be a wise man than to be a fool. One walks in safety while the other stumbles through life. But the wise man and the fool both have the same fate. There is no difference between them in that regard. They will both be brought down low by the grave.

So now we come to the real reason for Solomon's disenchantment with wisdom. He loved it, but it did not give him the happiness he desired. The reason is something surprising, something that was hidden from him while he was hot in wisdom's pursuit.

It was not wisdom itself he was seeking but something wisdom could not give him. The hidden reason why we want to build great things and obtain great wisdom is that we desire life. We desire an enduring identity, and we think such things can give us one.

Some words from the prophet seem revealing: "He will destroy in this mountain the face of the covering cast over all people, the veil that is spread over all nations. He will swallow up death in victory; and the Lord God will wipe away tears from off all faces."

Wipe away all tears? Doesn't that mean taking away our unhappiness? And how is this wonderful thing to be accomplished? By swallowing up death in victory; by taking away our humiliating defeat at the hands of the grave, our nakedness, and giving us life.

We may try to obtain this victory in human ways. We strive to succeed because we are attempting to overcome death. This applies not only to Solomon's building mania but to his feverish pursuit of wisdom. He can find wisdom in the ant, but the industrious little ant builds her own grave.

There was a veil covering his whole being. This veil made him think he could conquer death by conquering the world. The light had not yet come into the world to show him the astonishing truth. The way to conquer death is to die to the world.

The Great Reduction

*For there is no remembrance of the wise more than of the fool forever;
since all that is now shall in the days to come be forgotten.*

So now we know what's *really* troubling Solomon, what's got him down and feeling pessimistic about his accomplishments. It's the late-breaking realization that all striving is about identity, and yet all mortals must die and be forgotten. Therefore, all is vanity.

Those who feel offended when Solomon says such things must understand that he is not judging them or their successes. He is judging himself. He was the one who was determined to be great. And he was the one who finally realized those efforts were in vain.

Hidden in all of Solomon's great accomplishments was the desire to stand out. He did not realize this himself until he was old, as he plainly says. There was happiness in them while he was doing them because he thought they could make him happy.

But the fact that they did *not* make him happy has now revealed something to him: it was not really the fleeting feeling of happiness that he was looking for. It was immortality, which cannot be earned. This realization is the source of his bitterness, the same bitterness some find offensive.

Ecclesiastes is in the Bible to offend us and make us think seriously about life. Rabbis do things like that. And before we condemn Solomon for his pessimism, let us remember that he did not have the promise of life we are so fortunate as to enjoy.

He wrote an honest book about our prospects for making ourselves happy. It may be the most honest book ever written. All philosophers try to win us over by promising us we can obtain happiness in some form. Otherwise they cannot become popular.

But since we cannot give ourselves life, all philosophers tend to be liars.

The Great Reduction

Therefore I hated life; because the work that is wrought under the sun is grievous unto me: for all is vanity and vexation of spirit.

Do these words offend? Then how about this? "He that loves his life shall lose it; and he that hates his life in this world shall keep it unto eternal life." Those are the words of Jesus.

It seems we have to hate this mortal life in order to truly value eternal life. That's what we mean by "resistance," and that's what Ecclesiastes is all about. Solomon has begun to hate his life because he sees that it is mortal. It does not measure up to his expectations. It cannot give him peace.

But by the counterintuitive wisdom of the Bible, this is actually a good thing. If we are alienated from the world and its pursuit of fortune and fame, and have "no place to lay our heads," then it means we are not at home in the world—that is, at home with its vanity and foolishness.

Our innate resistance to those limitations gives us freedom. It also gives us a deep wisdom that the world cannot give. And in that case the extreme unhappiness seen in Ecclesiastes is nothing to be ashamed of. Identity sneaks in through the back door.

More from Jesus: "If the world hates you, know that it hated me before it hated you. If you were of the world, the world would love its own: but because you are not of the world, but I have chosen you out of the world, therefore the world hates you."

It sounds like some are *chosen* to experience the unhappiness Solomon is describing. It is an honor to be chosen. And they are hated by the world because their suffering exposes its shallowness, its vanity, just as Christ himself was hated by the world.

Unhappiness, as painful as it might be, can be good for us if it causes us to turn away from the world, which is perishing. Solomon is living through this process as he speaks.

The Great Reduction

I hated the labor I had done under the sun because I would have to leave it to the man who comes after me; and who knows if he will be a wise man or a fool?

Solomon's father said something quite similar: "Surely every man walks around in a vain show: surely they are disquieted in vain: he heaps up riches, and knows not who shall gather them."

And how many stories have we heard about this very thing in our own time, where someone accumulated great wealth only to have it squandered by careless offspring? Who has visited the mansions of Newport, all empty now, except for the blank-faced tourists?

It is a truism that success cannot be passed down. The father may revolutionize his industry, but it is highly unlikely that any of his sons will have the same talent or ambition. The mother may create her own highly successful travel business, but her daughters are unlikely to share her entrepreneurial gift.

Solomon saw all this, so it seemed to him that everything he had built was evanescent. It was not real; it had no permanence. His kingdom was in danger of being lost because he had to pass it on to someone who might not know what to do with it or might not care.

These words turned out to be prophetic. His son Rehoboam threatened to increase the tax burden with a foolish speech and wound up dividing Israel. The mighty kingdom built by David and maintained in peace by Solomon was gone in a flash.

We can find no peace in the great things we may have done once we realize they will not outlast us. Then it occurs to us that we have built our house on sand.

The Great Reduction

*I turned to cause my heart to despair regarding all the labor
I had undertaken under the sun.*

Despair! It is startling to see this word in the Bible. It stands out like a sore thumb. Ecclesiastes is a cry from the heart from someone who is very, very unhappy.

Solomon turned from a heart of joy to a heart of despair, not because his labors were inferior to others, but because his labors could not give him happiness or peace. Once he realized this, all hope was gone; which is the very definition of despair.

Solomon is actually living through the change he describes. We have seen other books of a similar kind. Augustine's *Confessions* comes to mind, and we are quite sure Augustine was thinking of Ecclesiastes when he wrote it.

Augustine had been living a pagan life, superficially happy in his misery, when suddenly something changed and caused him to turn to God. Solomon changed in the opposite direction, from rejoicing over his labors to despairing when he realized they were in vain.

One is a happy book; the other profoundly unhappy. One is about finding God; the other is about finding out the truth about ourselves. Both are different from the usual run of books because both authors are willing to be naked. They are not sermons; they are diaries.

Solomon's book is hard to read in youth, grows on you somewhat in middle age, and then, imperceptibly, becomes part of the very air you breathe. This shows that it was not written to garner popularity through the usual demographic. It was written to show us what we really are.

Actually it was written to glorify God. But we have a long way to go before we get there.

The Great Reduction

For there is a man whose labor is in wisdom and knowledge and equity; yet to a man that has not labored in these things he shall leave it for his portion.

Solomon might be able to find some comfort in all the great things he had accomplished if he had confidence he could leave them to a son or daughter who felt the same way—who was just like him and valued what he valued. But real life does not provide us with this comfort.

Our children have their own lives and identities. One of the great temptations of parenthood is to try to live through them. This shows our desire for perpetuating our own identity, but they cannot give us what we want because they are not us. They are a new creation.

Solomon believed in building his legacy with knowledge and wisdom and equity—in other words, in exactly the way he describes in Proverbs. And on the whole we can say that he did walk in the ways of the Lord, at least until he started turning away.

But here's the problem: there is no way for him to guarantee that his heirs will feel the same way about things. They may not possess the fortune he leaves them in uprightness. The identity he desires cannot be passed on with his inheritance.

In fact they may use their inheritance for debauchery or iniquity. In that case, not only is Solomon's good name not preserved through the worldly goods he passes on, but it is debased. We have seen many examples of this in our own time.

Once we realize that the riches we earn from our labors cannot make us happy for their own sake, we may convince ourselves that we can find happiness in the thought of passing them on to our children. Solomon shows us the vanity of this desire.

The Great Reduction

For what does a man have for all his labor, all the vexation of his heart, in which he has labored under the sun? All his days are sorrows, his travail grief; his heart does not take rest at night. This is also vanity.

If we are eager to be a success, to make a splash in the world, then there will be no rest from our labors; indeed, we will lie awake all night worrying about them.

Architect, are you sure you measured those windows perfectly in that fancy mansion? Accountant, are you sure you understood that new tax law? Engineer, do you really know what will happen to the load under those conditions? Surgeon, did you really stitch up that valve correctly?

By a strange twist of fate, the more we are driven by the need for perfection and success, the more restless our nights become. The thing that drives us also deprives us of our sleep and of peace. We thought success would bring us joy, but it can turn into desperation and even despair in the end.

And then there are the late nights of the "senior citizen." We know very well what it is to wake up in the middle of the night and not be able to go back to sleep. Our minds are racing. We try to turn them off but find we are powerless against the past . . . and the present.

The Great Reduction

There is nothing better for a man than that he should eat and drink, and that he should make his soul enjoy good in his labor.

So here is the first time Solomon makes this famous declaration, the great reduction, in its barest form. He will add some very important details later on, but for now let's consider what we have.

This admonition has been likened to Epicurus. It is very, very different. Epicurus believed that matter is all there is; in fact he inadvertently endowed matter with divine qualities by claiming that the universe must have created itself. This unconscious exaltation is the only possible basis for the idea that happiness can be found in matter for its own sake.

Food and drink are material things that give pleasure; therefore Epicurus reasoned that happiness, which he defined as tranquility of mind and freedom from fear of the grave, can be found in pleasing the stomach without doing it any harm. But Solomon has already tried that and found it wanting.

In fact Solomon's discussion of pleasure is the opposite of Epicureanism. He is not saying happiness can be found in moderate pleasures. He is saying happiness cannot be found, period. And *therefore* there is nothing better than to eat and drink and find satisfaction in our labors.

We are encouraged to seek contentment in these basic things, not because they are made of matter like us, but because they are gifts from God. Solomon doesn't say this—yet. But he doesn't have to. The great psalm says it for him: "You open your hands and satisfy the desires of every living thing."

The Bible is unique in proclaiming the goodness of God. "The Lord is good to all: and his tender mercies are over all his works." "O give thanks unto the Lord; for he is good: for his mercy endures forever." "For the Lord is good; his mercy is everlasting; and his truth endures to all generations."

It is Solomon's faith in God's goodness that lies behind his admonition to enjoy our meat and drink. Perhaps the thought of that goodness is the only thing keeping him from despair. Now, to enjoy good in one's labor is to enjoy labor that is good. Solomon will have more to say about this later on.

The Great Reduction

For who can eat, or who else can hasten here, more than I?

Is this self-deprecation? Solomon used to be in the rat race, as he has told us many times. He used to try to make himself great by building more things and accumulating more stuff and writing more proverbs and songs than anyone else.

But then he realized that none of these things were giving him the happiness he was seeking, and he also realized why—death was going to take them all away. He could not find the permanence, the identity, he was looking for in his mighty endeavors.

Solomon had been playing the comparison game. Then he had a sobering thought. He was no less mortal than anyone else. There is nothing lowlier than a grave, and by that measure he was just as naked as anyone. The comparison game lost its charm.

Now he pokes a little fun at himself, perhaps, by saying that at least no one can beat him to the dinner table. We have no special knowledge of Solomon's portions or proportions, but we can see why this comment might be amusing.

It used to be that he wanted to be first in the great things of the world. Now he is content to be first at recognizing the value of simple food and drink. Solomon's chastening is shown by this humble new form of hastening.

And perhaps we are not going too far if we speculate that there may be some prophetic meaning as well. After all, hastening to "the table" is good for us, isn't it?

The Great Reduction

*For God giveth to a man that is good in his sight wisdom,
and knowledge, and joy.*

To have wisdom and knowledge and joy, we must be good in God's sight. "Blessed is the man that walks not in the counsel of the ungodly, nor stands in the way of sinners, nor sits in the seat of the scornful. But his delight is in the law of the Lord; and in his law does he meditate day and night."

Goodness gives contentment. As unpleasant as it is to dwell on our transgressions, there is some complacency in remembering the good things we have done and are doing. Are we charitable? Just and merciful? Do we honor God? Stay humble? Strive to be kind to others? Live in peace with one another?

Isaiah 58 tells us that if we are charitable and do justice and take care of the widow and orphan and pay our workers then our light will "break forth as the morning, and your health shall spring forth speedily: and your righteousness shall go before you; the glory of the Lord shall be your reward."

True, Christ told the rich young man that "no one is good," but Christ also loved him when he told him he had obeyed the commandments from his youth. God does indeed smile favorably on those who strive to obey his holy law, even though they often fall short.

We smile on our own children when they are good in our sight. Why? Because we know that being good is good for them and for those they meet; we know that by being good they will be blessed, while at the same time we also know they are not perfect. It is no different with a heavenly Father.

Moses was right. It is not hard, generally speaking, to obey the commandments, certainly not impossible. And the wisdom of Proverbs still holds true. Those who do obey them will become wise and live much happier lives, while those who do not obey them will experience misery and darkness.

Can we obey them perfectly? Of course not. Jesus said, "Whoever is angry with his brother without cause shall be liable to judgment." Unwarranted anger violates the commandment, "You shall not kill." It is very unlikely that anyone can reach this level of perfection.

And yet it *is* perfectly possible to refrain from literally killing our neighbor. When we do, we give our neighbor life and are blessed. We find wisdom, knowledge, and joy. If for some horrible reason we are unable to refrain, and destroy life, then our own life will be in ruins, and there will be no joy.

It is also very possible to do all of the things listed by the psalmist, even though we are not good. It is possible not to walk in the counsel of the ungodly. It is possible not to stand in the way of sinners. It is possible not to sit in the seat of the scornful. None of these things are beyond our reach.

Jesus upset the young seeker by telling him that if he wanted to be *perfect* he had to sell all he had and give the money to the poor. But the wisdom Solomon is offering here is not about being perfect. It is about doing the best we can to live according to the law of love.

We obtain *wisdom* by so doing because we learn about the nature of God and the sweetness of goodness. We obtain *joy* because goodness brings life to others. Meanwhile those who willingly do evil cannot have these things. Riches they may have, and power, but the most important things elude them.

Do we have any reason to boast if we manage to be good in God's sight? Not at all. The commandments are there to reveal our nakedness. Solomon also makes it plain that no one is good. And he knew better than anyone. His lack of goodness is right out in the open for all to see.

In fact it seems likely to us that this is a statement of regret. Solomon has not been good in God's sight; far from it. He has married many wives and worshipped foreign gods and allowed detestable practices in Israel. And by his own account he does not have "wisdom, knowledge, and joy."

The Great Reduction

*But to the sinner he gives travail, to gather and to heap up,
that he may give to him that is good before God.
This also is vanity and vexation of spirit.*

Note he does not say the sinner *fails* to gather and heap up. He says his efforts are full of travail rather than wisdom and knowledge and joy, which are given to the one who is good in God's sight.

There can be no question that he does all of his gathering and heaping up for the sake of joy, because otherwise no one would do it. All our accumulating is based on the belief that it will make us happy. But instead of joy he finds vanity and vexation.

Can there be joy in any material thing? Momentary pleasure, yes, but lasting joy? Treasures on earth do not have such bewitching power. Joy can be found, however, in being good and in dwelling on the goodness of God. The thought of God's goodness brings us the joy the world cannot give.

The world has its haves and have-nots. The haves have money and nice homes and the have-nots are lacking these things. But the Bible has a very different view of haves and have-nots. The haves have joy in the Lord and the have-nots have travail and vexation.

Lest we be misunderstood, we do know that "no one is good" and no one can save himself through his goodness. But Solomon is talking about "good" in the ethical sense, not the moral. We are not good, but we can certainly do good. And when we do, God gives us wisdom, knowledge, and joy.

Is Solomon himself the sinner who travails and heaps up only to find that he has to leave it all to someone who is good in God's eyes? It certainly sounds like it. He descended into deep sin late in his life. It seems possible, then, that this very unhappy observation applies to his own situation.

The Great Reduction

*To every thing there is a season,
and a time to every purpose under heaven.*

This, of course, is one of the most beloved passages not just in Ecclesiastes but in the entire Bible. Many, many times we have heard these words read and pondered them in our hearts. They are far more familiar than anything found in Plato or Aristotle, and for good reason.

In one sense they deeply console us because they seem to speak of the sovereignty and goodness of God. It is a gift to have faith and not fear because in reality all of these things will happen in due season and over all of them there is the cast of divine benevolence.

But we think there may be an additional meaning in these soaring words for Solomon as well. All of these things have become rather wearisome to him.

A perverse way to read this passage is to think these are things God *wants* us to do. For example, Solomon tells us there is "a time to kill and a time to heal," but the commandments say "thou shalt not kill," and Jesus himself was a healer.

Now humans do kill, of course. They have wars. And they have times of healing and binding up. Solomon isn't necessarily making value judgments. But his point is that everyone has done them, and therefore they may not have the great significance we tend to assign to them.

There is a time to be born and a time to die. This is true of all people in all times and places. One's own individual birth or death is unique in the sense that it is his or hers—but so is everyone else's. To see this as it really is, is to be deprived of all vain notions.

Our lives are a story, and we are the hero of the story. This thought gives us joy because of identity. But Solomon in his old age has been deprived of this joy. There is nothing unique about the episodes of his life. They have been experienced before and will be experienced again.

An extra layer to his weariness is the underlying sense that these things have all been ordained. He cannot be the hero of his story if God is directing it. In that case everything he does is directed by God, not himself; heroism goes slinking away.

Worse, if God is directing all stories, then his own story is no longer a singularity. Every other life has value and significance in the eyes of God as well. Every other story has just as much value for that person as his own story does for him.

Or as we say today, it's not all about me. Such deep thoughts may be oppressive to those who are a little too full of themselves, which includes just about all of us.

The Great Reduction

What profit has he who works in that in which he labors?

If we take the preceding seven verses and put a colon after them, the context becomes clear. What is the point of all our endless striving if all of these things have been appointed? If the same things happen to all people that happen to you and to me, then why are we striving so hard and for what?

Well, we already know what. We are striving for identity, as Solomon is about to make clear.

The Great Reduction

I have seen the travail that God has given to the sons of men to be exercised in it.

Is it possible that the ennui Solomon is experiencing has been devised by God for his benefit? Does God give unhappiness to some in order to bring them back to the roost under his wing?

Adam's punishment was this: "Cursed is the ground for your sake; in sorrow you shall eat of it all the days of your life; thorns also and thistles shall it bring forth to you; and you shall eat the herb of the field; in the sweat of your face shall you eat bread, till you return unto the ground; for out of it were you taken: for dust you are, and unto dust you shall return."

Adam's sin was pride and wanting to make himself like God. His punishment was to toil in futility in order to learn that he is dust; to learn the difference between creature and Creator. But this is not punishment for the sake of punishment. Its purpose is to turn Adam (man) back to God.

Solomon has travailed mightily his whole life in an attempt to obtain a desirable identity, only to find unhappiness at the end of the road. Our travail has redeeming value, however, if it shows us the truth about ourselves and causes us to turn back to God.

Solomon has something very specific in mind—travail for the philosopher, whose efforts are just as futile as Adam's—as he is about to explain.

The Great Reduction

He has made everything beautiful in its time.

Nature is incomparably beautiful, deeply enjoyable, and Solomon concedes that God is the author of natural beauty, which is the most logical explanation for its existence. But nature's beauty can become a source of travail to someone like him in at least two ways.

First, as a *builder*. The beauty of nature gives such great pleasure that it inspires architects and artists to want to rise up to meet it. They want to make beautiful things and give pleasure themselves.

But such striving can become travail in the sense that it is impossible to overcome the difference between the overwhelming beauty of nature and our own rather stiff imitations. Try taking the greatest painting out of the museum and placing it in some natural setting to see what we mean.

Solomon cannot contend with God in creativity when making God's house; he cannot make a temple that rises up to the great pleasures of nature, even if he installs cedar paneling. Therefore it is possible for architects and builders to say that "all is vanity," if they are at all self-conscious.

But beauty can also become burdensome to a *philosopher*. Natural beauty strongly intimates the existence of a Creator who is good and full of delight, as Solomon acknowledges, but it is far beyond the reach of human wisdom. The greatness of nature's beauty exposes the limitations of philosophy.

Suffice it to say that the philosophers' notions of beauty are divided between sense and intellect. The lovers of pure intellect seek rational perfection by reducing beauty to simple forms—a circle, for instance. But circles lack the beauty of nature, and even at that they are not perfectly rational.

Meanwhile those who try to blend intellect and sense talk about "aesthetics" and are usually lovers of nature, but it is impossible to backfill their philosophy with beauty, which defies differential analysis. As soon as they start to describe their aesthetics, their powerlessness is exposed.

And then there are the philosophers of nothingness, the would-be heroes of humanism and god-slayers. For them, natural beauty is the hound of heaven. They can try to push painful questions about death and identity out of their minds through nihilism or merrymaking, but beauty prevents them.

Every time Solomon sees natural beauty he is reminded of God—and at the same time he is also reminded of the futility of his pursuit of wisdom.

The Great Reduction

He has set eternity in their heart.

More along the same lines, and perhaps the most important insight in Ecclesiastes regarding our continuing unhappiness. No one who has eternity in his or her heart can be satisfied with anything in the world because nothing we can do or have is eternal. All things are passing away.

Is Charlie the greatest home run hitter in the world? Pretty soon he will be too old to hit home runs, and then all the cheering will stop and he will be sitting at home wondering what to do with himself.

Is Jill a great and incomparable artist? She will find herself in competition with a great many other artists, not to mention agents, and her art is done on canvas in paint, which cannot last forever.

Is Randolph a great poet? In other cultures where other languages are spoken his greatness cannot be known, and even his own language will change, causing his greatness to fade away.

Is Elissa a great architect? Well, no need to go into her travail. Just ask Solomon. Nothing made of wood or brick or stone can last forever, not even with the mighty cedars of Lebanon.

If there is eternity in our hearts, then the difference between us and immortal God is exposed, and we see that all is vanity and we cannot obtain the identity we desire through our accomplishments. As James puts it, "What is your life? It is a vapor that appears for a little time and then vanishes."

And then he adds: "Draw nigh to God, and he will draw nigh to you. Cleanse your hands, you sinners; and purify your hearts, you double minded. Be afflicted, and mourn, and weep: let your laughter be turned to mourning, and your joy to heaviness."

Solomon could not have said it better. In fact he will say almost the same thing himself in a little while. But if we put the statement "he has made everything beautiful in its time" together with "he has put eternity in their hearts," we begin to understand his frustration and why all is vanity.

If nature is beautiful, then God will not let him go. Everything he sees reminds him of God. And if God has put eternity into his heart, then there is nothing he can do and no riches or wisdom he can obtain that will make him happy. God has made it impossible for him to be content with the world.

But what does it mean—"God has set eternity in their hearts"? It refers to the resistance Solomon is experiencing. The fact that he cannot be satisfied with the great things he has accomplished shows there is a hidden resistance in him to his own accomplishments. And this resistance reflects eternity.

This is Solomon's diagnosis of the human condition. If it resonates with us, then we might want to consider the following words from Christ: "If anyone thirsts, let him come unto me and drink. He that believes in me, as the scripture has said, out of his stomach will flow streams of living water."

Solomon thirsts—he is unhappy. He recognizes that the great beauty of nature and the eternity in his heart are hidden causes of this thirst. But such a thirst can only be quenched with life. Those streams of living water that come from Christ are the Spirit, who is the lord and giver of life.

Do we continue to thirst, in spite of all we have done? And do we know the *real cause* of our thirst? And if so, have we considered Christ in spite of the Christian religion, which so often stands in the way of drinking in his living water?

The Great Reduction

*No man can find out the work that God made
from the beginning to the end.*

The flip side of eternity is that it has no end and no beginning. We are conscious of beauty and have eternity in our hearts, but we are not eternal. This makes Solomon's heroic quest for wisdom impossible.

"God's thoughts are higher than our thoughts." This is becoming increasingly evident now in the field of medicine and molecular biology. There is a degree of complexity in the seemingly simplest of things that simply confounds human thinking.

The more we know, the more our opinions are divided. It wasn't supposed to be that way. The entire plan of modern science, as laid out by Bacon and Descartes, was to come to agreement about nature and thus to know the mind of God. "Science," after all, means knowledge.

And yet the mysteries that baffled from the beginning continue to baffle. What is light? What is gravity? What is magnetism? Why does the solar system mesh with perfection to nourish life on earth? How is it possible to see clearly and with consistency? What is consciousness? Most of all, what is "I"?

If you want to have your brain blown, go see what scientists have to say about the brain. They want to know why we think, why we learn, why we have memory. But these things are so fleeting and complex that they literally can only be described through metaphors.

In some ways science has become like the Tower of Babel. The more we try to find out the work God has made and make ourselves equal in understanding to God, the more we are divided. Solomon's lament is still meaningful for us today.

*I know that there is no good in them but for a man to rejoice
and to do good in his life.*

There is no good in the good things God has made for the poor person who is wracking his or her brains to understand them—in other words, no good result. Life is not long enough to understand what God has done from the beginning to the end.

They are very good in another sense, however—their goodness is a cause for enjoyment and rejoicing. "The heavens declare the glory of God, and the firmament shows forth his handiwork." The rejoicing heart, full of praise for what God has done, is uniquely happy.

Meanwhile all this goodness gives us a bright idea. Looking on what is good, and perceiving how much pleasure goodness gives, the mind is moved to value goodness. The mind makes a little leap and perceives there is value in being good.

And being good, to the extent we are able, is one thing that can certainly make us happy, as Solomon has already told us.

The Great Reduction

*And also that every man should eat and drink,
and enjoy the good of all his labor; it is the gift of God.*

Here is our great reduction again, but now he finally adds the all-important qualifier. Our eat and our drink are very good, not just for their own sake, and not because we are trying to push God out of our mind—which is impossible—but because they are a gift from God.

Think about honey. Do we make its sweetness or is it a gift? Think about milk. Is there any way it can be improved upon, right from the cow? Think about the egg. We do not lay it, but we love to eat it, sunny side up or over easy, and it is very good for us.

What about the summer peach plucked fresh from the tree? What about the plate of steamed string beans with fresh-ground pepper or the sun-ripened tomato or warm cucumber from the garden? Do we make them? Or do we pick them and enjoy them?

Yes, they are the good of our labor, if we planted and cultivated and harvested. It was labor for pure good, since it resulted in things that are good to eat and drink and caused us no frustration of the type Solomon has been experiencing.

Farming has never made anyone vain. Farming also keeps you close to the earth and its goodness, a perpetual source of pleasant reflection. And maybe most of all, farming compels you to bend a knee to the Creator, which is the road back to Eden.

This simple wisdom from Solomon comes at his own expense. His past labors to make himself great did not give him happiness. But it seems that happiness can be found in the grateful enjoyment of the good things that come from God, and in humility itself.

The Great Reduction

I know that, whatever God does, it shall be forever: nothing can be put to it, nor any thing taken from it: and God does it in order that men should fear before him.

Not only is it impossible for us to understand the work that God has made, but it is also impossible for us to add to or take anything away from it. Our pride is all nonsense.

Think for a moment about the earth revolving and rotating at certain necessary speeds—necessary for life—while the energy coming from the sun remains constant over vast expanses of time. What can be added to or taken away from this ingenious arrangement by our efforts to make a name for ourselves?

And yes, if we thought about these things at all seriously, we would certainly learn to fear God. The rotation of the earth only needs to slow a little bit in order for the whole system to fall apart. "The fear of the Lord is the beginning of wisdom."

The Great Reduction

That which has been is now; and that which is to be has already been; and God requires that which is past.

The familiar natural cycles that bring light and dark and rain and sun and seasons and harvests—these same cycles existed in the past just as we see them today, and they will continue to exist long after we are gone. God requires them. We call this "natural law," and it is fixed.

But in that case, what can even the greatest achievers do? What impact do all their accomplishments and striving have when we consider the omnipotence of God? How can they be full of themselves when God holds their fate in his hand?

Solomon has declared that "all is vanity." The great things he accomplished cannot give him a desirable identity because God has ordained all things from the beginning to the end. Nothing can be added, nothing taken away.

The more he tries, the more his nothingness is revealed to him. He has failed to obtain the immortal identity he desires. The vast expanses of time and workings of nature make this clear to him, things that are far beyond understanding.

The Great Reduction

And moreover I saw under the sun that there was wickedness in the place of judgment and iniquity in the place of righteousness.

Why is Solomon so unhappy and restless in his ripe old age? Partly it is because wisdom, the thing he loves the most, keeps showing him things he *really* does not want to see.

Our sense of psychological well-being depends very much upon the cheerful thought that all is right with our world (in general). This is the justice narrative. We cannot be happy, or at least not in the same way, if it occurs to us that this might not be the case.

The problem is identity. The love of country and church gives us a warm feeling as long as it makes us think well of ourselves—as long as we feel we are a part of something good. But this happiness fades if we begin to suspect wickedness in the place of judgment or iniquity in the place of righteousness.

The recognition of injustice in the courts and iniquity in the churches seems to have come to Solomon late in life. When that happens, the justice narrative we've been actively nurturing simply falls apart. One of our most important crutches for happiness is knocked out from under us.

This seems to be what has happened to Solomon. Why is he so unhappy? For one thing his justice narrative has been shattered and the vanity of his wisdom exposed.

The Great Reduction

I said in my heart, God shall judge the righteous and the wicked: for there is a time there for every purpose and for every work.

Solomon tries to fend off the happiness-shattering thought of injustice and iniquity by assuring himself that there is a righteous judge who will sort it all out in the end.

Wickedness may seem to prevail for reasons that are not clear to us from our mortal point of view. We want judgment to come faster, but it seems this is not part of God's plan. Instead, wickedness is allowed to continue in order for God's righteousness and justice to be revealed.

This is seen in the parable of the wheat and the tares. The workers—Solomon or us—want the weeds uprooted for the sake of identity, for vindication. But God says no; some wheat may be destroyed in the uprooting. Let them grow together until the harvest.

At the harvest, God, the righteous judge, will separate the wheat from the tares. Solomon avers that the thing he longs for will indeed happen. But there is a time and a place for everything, and man's justice is clumsy, and tends to kill the wheat along with the tares.

Solomon is looking for a philosophy to help him cope with his deep unhappiness. In this case, he uses the thought of the justice of God to counteract the devastating apprehension of injustice and iniquity. This stuff is not theoretical, and it is not religion. It is real.

And if we look at his father's psalms, we see a whole lot of coping of this nature. Many, many psalms beg for vindication of the righteous, of those faithful to God, and repudiation of the mockers, the willful evildoers, those who are bent on destruction and self-aggrandizement.

David would not have to beg if his need were not great. We think of Christ himself, surrounded by mockers and plotters, putatively the religious leaders of his own chosen people. He had the power to destroy them but did not. He left it for the Father to sort out.

The struggle is just as real for us today. Those who love God and honor goodness still see the rise of Pharisees and exploiters and willful evildoers of many kinds. It is not time yet for them to be judged. Identity cannot be sorted in the way we desire.

The waiting can be painful. Solomon's coping mechanism is useful for us because we can use it too. There are times in our lives when injustice and iniquity seem so thick that hope is lost. At those times we can remind ourselves, with Solomon, that there is another Judge.

"I said in my heart." Solomon is talking to himself. There are times when the key to lightening our burden is to imitate him and give ourselves a good talking-to. If we want to be at peace, then we need to remind ourselves from time to time to put our faith in God and his perfect justice.

Injustice and iniquity are not going away. Every new day provides another opportunity either to be outraged and depressed—or to benefit from the hard-won wisdom of Solomon and actively seek peace of mind in the sovereignty and justice of God.

The Great Reduction

I said in my heart concerning the estate of the sons of Adam,
that God might manifest them,
and that they might see that they themselves are beasts.

The commentators seem to want this to mean that Solomon is asking God to "manifest" or reveal to the wicked in the previous two verses that they are beastly, or perhaps have their wickedness revealed to all. In other words, they seem to be associating beastliness with wickedness.

We are inclined to think that Solomon is on to a new thought, however, and that the beastliness he has in mind has more to do with our mortality than morality. He seems to want God to make it very clear to "the sons of men"—that is, to all of us—that we are "beasts" in the sense that we are mortal.

If so, then this is about the difference between the creature and the Creator. We like to flatter ourselves that we are closer to the Creator than to the beasts. How many times have we seen philosophers compliment themselves over the difference between them and the beasts, which is reason?

They think reason makes them like God, but the big divide between us and God is our mortality, and in that sense we are no different from the beasts. We are all made of dust, and to dust we shall return. This shocking thought is Solomon's way of curing us of our insufferable vanity.

If we are looking for a tie-in to the previous verses, then it might be that we are very vain to think we can separate the wheat from the chaff. To have our beastliness manifested to us—our mortality—is to be cured of this singular delusion and obtain some degree of peace.

> *For that which befalls men also befalls beasts;*
> *as one dies, so dies the other.*

Solomon is wishing here for a full manifestation to himself that he is no less mortal than the beasts. He is not God. He cannot live forever. He cannot separate the wheat from the chaff. He should not be so much in love with the sword of judgment, which also cuts those who wield it.

Solomon hopes for his own limitations to be revealed to him so that he can set aside the thing standing between him and God, between him and contentment, which is his foolish pride. He is actively lobbying for his own pride to be destroyed, even against his will.

We can't help wanting to be like God, as children of Adam and Eve, but this desire is vanity and a trap because we are not God. We can't rectify the world or do away with iniquity and injustice. We can't even do away with them in ourselves, as Paul points out.

If we cling to pride, we will be unhappy. As a philosopher of contentment, Solomon recommends that we take a good hard look at ourselves and realize we are made of dust. And then pride goes away.

The Great Reduction

Wherefore I perceive that there is nothing better than that a man should rejoice in his own works; for that is his portion: for who shall bring him to see what shall be after him?

If we are made of dust like the beasts, then where are we most likely to find contentment? Not in playing God and attempting to separate the wicked from the righteous.

We can find joy in our own work because we were made to work, according to Solomon. This is one of his key insights. The problem comes when we try to make our identity contingent upon our works, when we try to boast in them. And then our works can never make us happy.

This is true of Solomon and his mighty works. If he is focused on their ability to make him "great," then they cannot give him peace. But if he rejoices in those works for their own sake—in the pleasure of work itself, which is a gift from God—then he can have contentment and even joy.

The same can be said of anyone who works, not just makers of great buildings. Work is their portion. This is what God has kindly given them to do. To do honest work with all of their heart is to find contentment in their work, the contentment that seems to have eluded Solomon.

Those who work with their hands also need to be philosophers from time to time. They need to remind themselves to be content. They need to remind themselves that their work—as well as their enjoyment of it—are gifts from God and be grateful.

They are not trying to echo the greatness of their work down through the ages, as Solomon has done. How can that make you happy? Who is going to bring you to see what comes after you? Once you're dead, you're dead; there's no more satisfaction in your work.

And by the way, the "works" referred to here have nothing to do with the good works that become a bone of contention in Paul. Solomon is *not* saying we can save ourselves through our works. He is saying we can find contentment in the productive work God has given us to do.

The worker who knows how to be content with his work can have peace, but Solomon cannot have peace as long as he is looking to the future with his great works.

So I returned and considered all the oppressions that are done under the sun: see the tears of the oppressed, and they had no comforter; and on the side of their oppressors there was power, but they had no comforter.

He returns from the happy thought of the calming effect of our work to the various injustices that are driving him to distraction. This time it is the tears of the oppressed, tears you can taste, once you have acknowledged they exist and are in fact a condition of existence.

Those salt tears have corrosive power. They dissolve the chirpy story of happiness we have been telling ourselves all along. If we have seen their tears, then we cannot be happy, because we know the story is false. If we know they are oppressed, then we cannot be free.

On the side of their oppressors there was *power*. This is extremely disconcerting, once grasped. What is, is not necessarily right. God is sovereign, but the world has sovereigns of its own, and they may oppress their people with apparent impunity.

And the oppressed have no comforter! Solomon was thinking of himself, his hero-image. He sees the oppressed in neighboring lands and is driven to distraction by their tears, but there is nothing he can do about it. He wants to be their comforter but does not have that power.

Now in his defense it should be noted that he was a peacemaker. He did not attack neighboring lands or meddle in their affairs, as his father chronically did. The fact that he felt powerless in spite of his armada of chariots has more to do with an unwillingness to do battle than the inability.

But the point is that Solomon is still on the same dispiriting theme as above. There is endemic injustice in the world, and this injustice takes away his happiness. As it should. No person of conscience or worth should be happy when they think of the tears of the oppressed and the injustices of power.

People who are ruled by a wicked king must simply endure his wickedness. No superhero is going to come along and save them or remove their chains. They were born in those chains, and they will also die in them, and so will their children in all likelihood.

The Great Reduction

If we are superheroes in our own minds, as was Solomon, wise folk on the side of good, perhaps wearing a cape, then to know such things is to taste their tears and our own limitations at the same time.

The Great Reduction

*Therefore I praised the dead which are already dead
more than the living which are yet alive.*

It is not the purpose of this dark reflection to cause us to envy the dead. Its purpose is to show us just how unhappy Solomon actually is. He is starting to envy the dead because the dead feel no pain. It is his own pain that is making him envy the dead.

This self-annihilating pain makes all of the other pieces fall into place. It is not hard to understand how someone who is in as much pain as Solomon might be moved to have an outburst like "all is vanity." It is not hard to understand his disillusionment with the world.

To praise the dead, to envy them for their peace, establishes his good faith. There is no vanity or hypocrisy in him. He is speaking from the heart. He tried to clothe himself in wisdom, but now he is so very unhappy that he wonders if he might be better off dead.

A comforter is coming. "Comfort, comfort ye my people." But Israel will have to endure a great deal of self-inflicted suffering in the meantime, more even than Solomon can imagine; although, as we know, he was partly the cause of it.

The Great Reduction

Yes, better off than both of them is he who has not yet been, who has not seen the evil work that is done under the sun.

Solomon recapitulates his theme. He has seen the evil done under the sun, and it is so painful to him that he almost wishes he had never been born.

Again, this painful wisdom is late-breaking. This same Solomon was the author of the sunny Proverbs, but what he has seen makes sunniness impossible. He has become aware of the reality of evil, of the dark shadows of being, and this awareness oppresses him terribly.

Humility of the profoundest type has come to a man who wishes he had never been born. Solomon's justice narrative has been destroyed, and his vaunted wisdom seems like nothing to him now.

Again, I considered all travail, and every right work—and for this a man is envied of his neighbor. This is also vanity and vexation of spirit.

Now he moves on to another painful thought. Call it the curse of the gifted. They work hard and excel and do things right only to find that they are envied.

When we see the symphony orchestra smiling benignly at the soloist, we may think they are happy for him or her. That's definitely what they want us to think. But in fact most of them are envious of soloists and wish they could be standing in their place. This is human nature.

Are you sure you want that president's award you've been coveting? It will probably cause others to hate you and want to put you in your place. Achievement cannot give happiness because it cannot give us the genuine admiration we are seeking.

Do you want to build that beautiful house with the beautiful gardens? You may be disappointed. The more beautiful your house and gardens become the more likely others will be to envy you and wish they could topple you from your high horse.

Envy takes away the joy of achievement. What we are really looking for in achievement is love, affirmation; but the more we achieve, the more we encounter resistance. Human nature makes it impossible for us to obtain the thing we desire the most.

Envy also makes achievement a trap and a burden. Today's great successes must be followed up by even greater successes tomorrow. And then old age comes along and takes all achievement away.

The Great Reduction

The fool folds his hands together, and eats his own flesh.

But of course this is not a recommendation for nothing-doing. Achievement cannot make us happy because of envy, but neither can idleness, since one of Solomon's key insights is that we have been *made* to work and to find contentment in our work.

Wisdom is a two-edged sword. If we desire contentment, then is it not enough to see through the vanity of our desire for achievement; we must also see through the vanity of the opposite, which is the facile celebration of cynicism and sloth.

The fool who folds his hands together eats his own flesh if his flesh was made for work, as Solomon contends. There is satisfaction in working with his hands, which have been exquisitely made for that purpose. To fold them in idleness is to eat himself.

We have seen these verses described as indicative of a golden mean between the extremes of overachieving and the foolishness of nothing-doing. This is undoubtedly true, but for us the key insight is that we have been made to work.

To know the secret of contentment requires knowing the secret of how and why we were made, of what we truly are. Solomon is plumbing these great mysteries for us.

The Great Reduction

*Better is a handful with quietness than both hands full
with travail and vexation of spirit.*

At one time in his life he was raucously campaigning for happiness through overachieving. Now it seems to him, having been chastened, that nothing is more valuable than simple peace of mind.

This is a great revelation. It is easy to set aside the need for quietness when we are young and full of energy but impossible when we are old and can no longer distract ourselves through endless activity. It now occurs to Solomon that quietness is what he was seeking all along. He just didn't realize it.

Happiness is a restless state; quietness is contentment. Happiness is based on moving the world; quietness comes most of all from the thought of God and his goodness. Happiness can only be pursued, never grasped; quietness is at hand for those who have faith.

"He makes me to lie down in green pastures. He leads me beside the still waters." This is a picture of the quietness Solomon has in mind. There is a reason why these are two of the most beloved sentences in all literature.

The Great Reduction

Then I returned, and I saw vanity under the sun.

Returned from where? From foreign lands, where he saw the tears of the oppressed? From the sunny state of mind he had momentarily obtained when, through the power of philosophy, he invoked the blessed state of quietude? Yes, and yes.

This book is about the return of unhappiness. It can be pushed off. It can be pushed out. But it cannot be pushed aside. We can go here and there in our minds, and sometimes have happiness, but the unhappiness of the human condition is not something we can escape.

Solomon has returned to unhappiness many times in his life, as described, but now he is realizing that unhappiness *always* returns. It may go away for a while, but it is coming back with a vengeance. There is no way to escape suffering. It is part of being human.

Unlike the philosophers, he is no longer pretending that it is possible to be happy. But how can we make progress if we refuse to be honest about ourselves?

The Great Reduction

There is one alone, and there is not a second; indeed, he has neither child nor brother: yet is there no end of all his labor; neither is his eye satisfied with riches; and neither does he say, For whom do I labor and bereave my soul of good? This is also vanity, yes, it is a sore travail.

Ecclesiastes is a philosophy practicum. Philosophy is not really the love of wisdom if it is not tested in the real world. And if all our philosophy cannot bring us quietude, then it is vanity.

In the real world, it is not good to be alone. Men and women were made for fellowship. The quietude we desire is impossible in solitude. To be in solitude is to be filled with solicitude. The mind races with no way to find a landing place.

"How sweet it is when the brothers live together in unity." And how bitter it is when the brothers live together in disunity. And how lonely it is when a brother, torn between unity and disunity, decides it is better to go it alone.

In the case in question, this brother is attempting to fill the void with work and accumulation. There is a hole in his heart called loneliness which he is trying to fill with money. But this particular hole cannot be filled with anything other than another.

As we see in Scrooge, loneliness can become a self-fulfilling prophecy. If we try to fill the void with work and money, in time we may reach a state where we are afraid to intermingle. We become so set in our solitary ways that it is hard to contemplate the idea of letting others in.

A successful woman recently confessed in a major newspaper that she was very lonely. She had sacrificed relationships for the sake of a career and competing with men. Now she had to face the prospect of always being alone and having no one to comfort her in her old age.

She wondered if it was too late to change because she had become too set in her ways. She did not know if she was even capable of living with someone else after living alone for so long. Fear had taken over and hidden itself as toughness and indifference and success.

She was the person in Solomon's example, a prisoner of her own ambition. She had gained a glorious isolation which did not seem so glorious from the inside. She saw herself in old age with no mate and no children to care for her or about her. And she was depressed.

All our high-flying ideas about things must be tested in real life. It may seem terribly mundane to think about old age and having no children to cheer us or care for us, but this is what life actually is, as opposed to what we may want it to be.

This is not to judge her by any means. It is simply to point out that the choices we make can send us tumbling in directions we did not anticipate and may not find very gratifying.

The Great Reduction

Two are better than one; because they have a good reward for their labor.

There are two kinds of profundity. There is faux profundity, where someone tries to impress us by making his pronouncements seem difficult and obscure. The very fact that they are obscure makes them seem profound, but their profundity is usually an illusion.

There is no profundity of that kind in Ecclesiastes. Instead there are observations like this one that are not intended to glorify the philosopher or magnify his genius but rather to equip the mind with the wisdom it needs to find quietude in an electric world.

Among the innumerable thoughts and ideas to be sorted by the mind in its search for contentment is the simple truth that two are better than one. But here's the thing about this simple truth. It may seem rather self-evident, but its self-evidence does not come into being until it is said.

The expression of this supremely simple truth shows a reducing process at work in Solomon, like the production of a fine sauce. There was a time when he was not unlike the philosophers. He too eagerly sought the identity of a lover of wisdom, one of the sweetest identities known in this life.

His Song of Songs is full of wondrous things that are very strange and difficult to understand. It may be the hardest book to interpret in the whole Bible. Those who refer to it as an erotic love poem are only fooling themselves. If so, the rabbis would not have loved it so much or put it in their holy book.

But now Solomon has seen that "all is vanity." He no longer aspires to the mantle of inscrutability or ecstatic verse. His concern is to deal with the unhappiness of the present moment, and this makes him very prosaic. When something real is in play, we are no longer in the mood for dancing.

The wisdom being imparted here is very much like his insight about the value of work. It is a question of how we were made. Genesis tells us we were made for companionship with God and with each other. If true, then this is extremely important information for those who are seeking contentment.

The Great Reduction

No one is elevated in the world by observing that two are better than one. But true philosophy is about finding contentment, and in that sense Solomon is the truest and most reliable philosopher.

The Great Reduction

For if they fall, the one will lift up his fellow: but woe to him that is alone when he falls; for he does not have another to help him up.

Now of course this does not just refer to physical falls but to all the various types of pratfalls that are experienced in life. It is not difficult to lift ourselves up from a physical fall, but there are other types of falls from which it can be very hard to rise.

If we are alone, then we must bear these falls alone, without having the consolation of fellowship to comfort us, the love of a friend. Worse, we must bear them without the perspective obtained only from fellowship, that falls are common to the human race.

We are all human; we all fall. But woe to those who fall alone and have no one to help them up when they fall. Not only is there damage in the fall itself, but there is deeper damage in the psychological fallout, the self-abuse that comes with falling short of our own ideal.

Solitary heroes labor under a terrible burden. They are no better than anyone else, no less prone to falls in the realms of business, morals, or ethics, but they must bear the psychological fallout from those falls by themselves, which can only be done through a process of hardening.

The problem with this hardening process is that it divests us of our humanity. The solitary hero tries to chisel himself in stone, but human hearts are made of flesh and blood, and long for love.

The Great Reduction

Again, if two lie together, then they have heat: but how can one be warm?

Let's talk about the hardening just described for a moment. It is cold, and we were made warm-blooded and are naturally attracted to the warmth provided by relationships.

But what is this warmth? The reason for the warm bond seen in families is not blood but identity. The natural love they feel for their kin is linked to kind. Family love kindles them because it gives them a sense of being, belonging; and where there is no kinship there can be no warmth.

Outside of the family, two are warm because it is only in the other that identity and being are disclosed. Two sticks rubbed together generate warmth, but one alone remains in its unkindled state. Kindling requires coming into contact with another.

Marriage is said to reflect our relationship with God, but that relationship can be either warm or cold. If we say to ourselves that warm is better than cold, just as we like the down quilt on a cold night better than a bare sheet, then certain concessions must be made for the sake of contentment.

Coming together for warmth is not always easy. We are selfish beings by nature who want our own way and our own gratification. Laying down those selfish desires for the sake of warmth requires us to make choices, and choices require right thinking. That's where philosophy comes in.

The Great Reduction

*And if one prevail against him, two shall withstand him;
and a threefold cord is not quickly broken.*

The million-dollar question is, who is "him"? It could be an obnoxious neighbor, but we have someone much more insidious in mind, someone with a relentless desire to destroy us.

Two shall withstand him because they lift each other up. Two shall withstand him because they keep each other warm and encourage one another. Two shall withstand him because the bond they share was forged by God and *love is stronger than death.*

Which brings us to the threefold cord. There is no need to do more than to acknowledge what many commentators have already written. When God is added to the bond it becomes unbreakable. And it also reflects another unbreakable bond, the greatest one of all.

The Great Reduction

Better is a poor and a wise child than an old and foolish king, who will no more be admonished.

We will speculate that this refers to himself and his father. His father was a poor and wise child, and Solomon has become an old and foolish king who will no longer listen to good counsel.

Like Solomon, many of us have found ourselves no longer full of the promise of youth, which now seems like an illusion. Time has robbed us of that infantile joy. Solomon has grown old and foolish in many ways, according to his own words.

The young self, full of vitality and dreams of happiness—because that's what we all dream about—gives way to the old, fumbling at the door, knowing ourselves too well, wondering if "all is vanity," since we have not found happiness.

The real obstacle to happiness is ourselves. We simply are not the heroes we would like to be. A poor and wise child is better off than the old king because he is still a blank slate, still moldable and full of hope. For the wizened king, all hope for happiness is gone.

The child is innocent; the king, not so much. The child has done nothing to mar his identity; the king has chased after foreign wives and worshipped their gods. The burden of old age is that the past cannot be changed.

Solomon's father, on his deathbed, declared justice to be the shining attribute of a king. He was a "poor and wise child" that Samuel chose from among many more promising brothers. His wisdom is clearly seen in his many and varied psalms.

Solomon had other things on his mind, however. A man with seven hundred wives may seem powerful, but he cannot be at peace. Consequently Solomon's famous last words will not be glowing or poetic. They are the unhappy book he is writing right now.

The Great Reduction

For out of prison he comes to reign, while he that is born in his kingdom [born a king] becomes poor.

The "he" that comes out of prison is the poor but wise child—David (in our interpretation)—while the "he" that is born a king is the foolish old king—Solomon himself.

The poor but wise boy comes out of his poverty, a type of prison, to become king. His arc is ascending, although there were certainly some bumps along the way. David's last words are those of a man who seems generally content with his life and what he has done.

Solomon's arc, however, is in the opposite direction. He was born a king, but he is headed downward into a prison of his own devising. Unwise choices have led to the psychological box in which he now finds himself, a prison that cannot be escaped.

We pity the poor child for the prison of poverty in which he was born when perhaps we should be pitying the child who is born a king and finds himself in a prison of a different kind.

The Great Reduction

I considered all the living who walk under the sun, with the second child that shall stand up in his stead. There is no end of all the people, even of all that have been before them: and they that come after shall not rejoice in him. Surely this also is vanity and vexation of spirit.

Solomon was not the first person to have this thought. Here is his father: "Behold, you have made my days as a handbreadth; and my age is as nothing before you: truly every man at his best state is altogether vanity."

Solomon is the second child, standing up in the stead of his illustrious predecessor, trying to equal him in the eyes of the world with all his wisdom and his works and his amassed wealth and thousand songs and wives and concubines.

Moreover he is the king. While he lives, he has the whole world at his feet. The nation of Israel invested its identity heavily in the king. That was why they wanted a king in the first place—and why we still have a soft spot in our heart for the peculiar breed today.

But suddenly Solomon has a vision of the endless procession of mortals on this earth, and his identity becomes like water. In their tiny orbit he and his father may seem great, but in the whole vast scheme of things they too are nothing and their greatness has no substance.

The king draws identity from the love of his people. His greatness is obtained through their adulation. But it now occurs to Solomon that this greatness is nothing but a bubble, since all of those admirers will eventually pass away.

As we speak, our children are forgetting the adulation that once attended our former leaders. Presidents who seemed larger than life become bland faces in a history book. Solomon sees this now in his old age, and it vexes his spirit; his nothingness oppresses him.

The Great Reduction

*Keep your foot when you go into the house of God,
and be more ready to hear than to give the sacrifice of fools:
for they do not consider that they do evil.*

Solomon has just had a harrowing apprehension of the unrelenting march of time and the dissolution of being. Having lost his footing, he now returns to the house of God determined to "keep his foot"; to the only place where he can find peace.

Maybe he was thinking of his father's great psalm—"One thing have I desired of the Lord, that will I seek after; that I may dwell in the house of the Lord all the days of my life, to behold the beauty of the Lord, and to enquire in his temple."

When you are in great need, *how* you go into the Lord's house is very important. All pride and vanity must be put aside, because you are, after all, a supplicant. To keep your foot is to go in with your head bowed down so your heart can be uplifted.

We go because we need to hear from God, not because God needs to hear from us. God's word is a lamp unto our feet; our words fall into darkness, as Solomon has just seen. Therefore put aside the vain desire to make oneself heard, the sacrifice of fools.

God has prepared a sanctuary for us where we can go to meet him. He no longer dwells in this sanctuary in the sense that he dwelt in the tabernacle, in the cloud between the cherubim; therefore the meeting must be appointed in our minds.

The reason God does not dwell in his house anymore is that he has come and dwelt among us. "Keep your foot" has a whole new meaning for New Testament believers. We come to seek the "unity of the Spirit through the bond of peace."

Meeting God in the sanctuary today means meeting him in the mystery of mutual, self-sacrificing love. This requires preparation of the mind. We see the humility Christ showed when he submitted to the cross, and we imitate this humility in our fellowship.

This is shown in the great parable of the Pharisee and the publican. It is not our boasting about our righteousness that makes us right with God but humility and sorrow for our sins. That is the way to enter God's house and find rest.

Just as Christ had to keep his feet when he carried his cross through the cobbled streets of Jerusalem, so we must keep our feet when we carry our own cross into the house of God.

The Great Reduction

Do not be rash with your mouth, and do not let your heart be hasty to utter anything before God: for God is in heaven, and you are on earth: therefore let your words be few.

Why should we restrain the tongue when we go into the house of the Lord? First of all, it would be presumptuous to do otherwise. Who are we to talk to God?

Now of course this does not refer to the humble prayer offered in silence. It refers to the kind of talking we do when we are trying to impress others with our wisdom, like Job's friends, or like the Pharisee praying on the street corner for all to see.

In fact it seems quite possible that the instruction Solomon is giving here is for himself. We can imagine him having done quite a bit of talking in God's house, the one he himself built, since he thought he was wise, and now regretting it in his chastened state as he realizes his nothingness.

Self-reproach leads to a desire to zip the lips. When we've seen ourselves as we really are, we lose some of the joy we otherwise find in making our opinions known, especially on religious matters. We can hide our flaws from others but not from ourselves.

God's word is precious. It brings life and refreshment. Those who have been knocked down flat can be picked up again and put on their feet. But first they must hold their tongues.

The Great Reduction

For as a dream comes through the multitude of business,
so a fool's voice is known by a multitude of words.

This refers to the bad dreams we have when we are worrying about the multitude of problems we have at work or in life. Such dreams are useless and distressing; and so too is a fool, who is known by the multitude of his words. His words are like a bad dream.

The Great Reduction

When you make a vow to God, do not delay in paying it, for he has no pleasure in fools. Pay what you have vowed. It is better that you should not vow than that you should vow and not pay.

Following on the previous thought, Solomon cautions those who do have loose lips in the house of the Lord to be sure to make good on any vow they might make to God.

The problem is we are notoriously bad at keeping our vows. Joshua said, "As for me and my house, we will serve the Lord"—and the people wholeheartedly agreed. But they did not remain true to their vows. And for breaking them they were severely punished.

What is a vow? It is an attempt to show there is something in us that is more than mortal and changeable. But we have difficulty keeping our vows because we are in fact mortal. Paul writes that we live in "bondage to the grave"; among other things, this means it is very difficult for us to keep our vows.

A brilliant example from literature is John Dashwood, vowing to his father that he would obey his wishes and liberally take care of his stepmother and half-sisters, and then allowing himself to be talked out of it by his wife, who convinces him it is actually more charitable to leave them to their own devices.

John makes the vow as a signpost against his father's impending death, a show of resolve in the face of mortality, but his commitment soon wears away. What makes the example powerful is not that we are better than John Dashwood, but that we recognize something in him that is universally human.

Moses said this about making vows: "When you vow a vow unto the Lord your God, you shall not be slack to pay it: for the Lord your God will surely require it of you; and it would be sin in you. But if you forbear to vow, it shall be no sin in you."

But Christ said this: "You have heard that it has been said by them of old, You shall not forswear yourself, but shall perform unto the Lord your oaths: but I say to you, do not swear at all; not by heaven, for it is God's throne; not by the earth, for it is his footstool; nor by Jerusalem, for it is the city of the great King. Neither shall you swear by your head, because you cannot make one hair white or black. But let your communication be, yes, yes—or no, no. For whatever is more than these comes of evil."

That is, of pride. Christ is thinking of vows on a deeper level than Moses. It is our prideful nature and desire to distinguish ourselves that causes us to want to make vows in the first place. And as Solomon informs us elsewhere, pride goes before a fall.

Do not allow your mouth to cause your flesh to sin; and do not say before the angel that it was an error: so why should God be angry at your voice and destroy the work of your hands? For in the multitude of dreams and many words there are also many vanities: but you, fear God.

Can we talk our guardian angel into releasing us from any vow we have made? No, because the nature of a vow is that we cannot be released from it. When we vow, we assume a godlike mantle; and if we fail, we pay the price for our presumption.

Let us not attempt to blame the consequences for vow-breaking on God! We were told not to make a vow, and we went ahead and made one anyway; and now we must pay the price for our vanity, for trying to obtain identity by showing immortal resolve.

The multitude of words and dreams is human existence. We make vows because we are in love with our own words and because we are not realistic about our limitations. To fear God is to fear the consequences that may come with breaking our vows.

This is true most of all in the Lord's house. We go there seeking restoration of identity in his majesty and glory. We go there seeking peace. Our bumptious vows only stand in the way.

The Great Reduction

If you see the oppression of the poor, and violent perverting of judgment and justice in a province, do not marvel at the matter: for he that is higher than the highest is watching; and there are higher than they.

It disturbs Solomon to have suddenly become conscious of the tears of the oppressed at his late age, to have his justice narrative shattered. Here he tries to use philosophy to talk himself out of being so disturbed that the will is neutralized.

He tries to rationalize oppression and injustice, not to excuse them by any means, but to give himself the means of carrying on and staying sane in spite of them. Remember, he was so vexed by them that at one point he literally wished he had never been born.

The traditional way to read this is that God and the angels, or perhaps the triune God, see the oppression. This thought salves the wound by assuring us that God's justice will prevail in the end, although the words don't seem to fit the explanation very well.

Another possibility that has been mentioned is that the ones doing the oppressing also have overlords and are themselves being oppressed. This either makes us pity them or rejoice in the thought that they may be suffering as much as their victims.

In either case, it is not clear how much consolation such a rationalization can provide. Oppression and injustice do not go away. We can use a rationalization to cover our wound, but if the wound is not healed then we are going to need a new rationalization tomorrow.

The Great Reduction

He that loves silver shall not be satisfied with silver;
nor he that loves abundance with increase: this is also vanity.

This principle may be more important today, in an age of great affluence, than it has ever been. The thirst that we have—whatever it is—cannot be satisfied with material things.

The proof that God has set eternity in our hearts is this: he who is in love with silver cannot be satisfied with silver. If he is in love with it, then why shouldn't a large quantity of it make him happy? The reason is there is something more to this love of his, this restless desire.

There is something lying behind his love of silver, concealed from him, which is his desire for identity. And there is even something lying behind that, which is a thirst for life. The thirst for identity cannot be satisfied with anything that does not give us life.

The same principle applies to abundance. It is not abundance for its own sake that we want—although we think it is—no, it is the power of abundance to substantiate identity. Abundance cannot give us happiness or contentment because of a desire that is hidden from our own eyes.

Solomon is not moralizing. He is reporting. He is the man who accumulated vast quantities of silver and great abundance. But he's beginning to realize that only one thing can satisfy his thirst.

The Great Reduction

When goods increase, they are increased that eat them: and what good is there to the owners thereof, saving the beholding of them with their eyes?

Solomon kvetches about the plight of great men with great households in the ancient world. One reason why silver and abundance cannot satisfy them is that the more these things increase the more their dependents increase to consume them.

For those of us who are not great landowners with great households, there may be another application. Silver and abundance cannot satisfy us because as they increase so do our goods. It's human nature. We tend to upgrade. We get a raise, so we buy a bigger house, a slicker car, the latest iPhone.

Someone did a survey once and was struck by the finding that people across all economic strata felt they could be happy if they only had twenty percent more income. There was no difference between rich and poor on that score. They all thought they needed just a little more.

This hope is an illusion, because as their income increases so do their obligations. If they took the extra twenty percent and saved it, that would be one thing; but the natural inclination is to spend it, to increase their goods, and thus to increase their expenses and their stress.

In either case, the message is this: it is better to be content with what you have. Do not love silver because if you do you will never have enough. Those who heed this wisdom are much more likely to be happy than those who do not.

The sleep of a laborer is sweet, whether he eats little or much:
but the abundance of the rich will not suffer him to sleep.

The complaint about silver leads Solomon to see a great irony. The laborer who lacks abundance may have the very thing the rich man longs for and cannot have: a sweet night's sleep.

Laborers sleep well because they are weary from their labors. They have contentment. They have simplicity. They do not have a horde of dependents. They are not tossing and turning at night thinking about silver because they don't have any silver to think about.

This is not the case with rich men like Solomon, however. If they have silver and abundance then they will have many things to worry about late at night on their beds. The riches Solomon so ardently desired become counterproductive when they prevent him from having a good night's sleep.

Is there anything that can make us feel more utterly helpless and miserable than the inability to get to sleep? That's when our powerlessness is truly revealed to us. There is nothing we can do about insomnia short of medicating ourselves, which has its own drawbacks.

A sweet night's sleep is something almost everyone desires, and insomnia is something almost everyone dreads, since it deprives us of rest. Therefore it is highly ironic that the simple laborer who has nothing can sleep at night while the rich king tosses restlessly on his soft bed.

By comparing himself unfavorably with a lowly laborer, Solomon is heading toward a realization of the value of simplicity and trust in God. These are the things that are most likely to bring peace.

The Great Reduction

There is a sore evil which I have seen under the sun, namely, riches kept for the owners to their hurt. But those riches perish by evil travail: and he has a son, and there is nothing in his hand.

Not only is it impossible for us to be satisfied with our riches, but they may do us actual harm.

For instance, the riches we desire so much may make us an object of envy and machinations on the part of others. It sounds like a man known to Solomon has made some enemies while amassing or inheriting his riches, and those enemies may have found a way to take their revenge.

Or it is possible that this fellow has lost his riches through some misstep of his own or general misfortune. It is just as easy to lose a fortune as it is to gain it. Many who were rich and heedless of the wrath of God in 1928 had no idea of the calamity that awaited them.

In any case, his riches have been taken away from him by some sort of evil travail—and he has a son to support. Worse than losing our riches is the humiliation of not being able to support our children, and worse yet is losing face in the eyes of our children.

Riches may hurt their owners in other ways as well. How many rich people have outsized problems with their children? How many find themselves hanging on at the end of life knowing that the smiling children at their bedside really want them to die so they can open the will?

"It is easier for a camel to go through the eye of a needle than for a rich man to enter into the kingdom of heaven." The kingdom referred to is peace and contentment, and the riches they desire may stand between them and this heavenly kingdom.

Their riches may change them for the worse. They may harden them to the plight of the poor and deprive them of pity and tenderness. They may make them proud and cause them to treat others with scorn or condescension, as we see in James. They may dim the *beautiful love* of justice and mercy.

If the rich believe they are saved by their riches, then they are sorely mistaken. They may have power, they may have influence; but blessed are the poor who know that only God can give them peace.

As he came forth of his mother's womb, naked shall he return to go as he came, and shall take nothing of his labor that he may carry away in his hand.

The poor fellow from the previous example who has lost his silver and abundance must go to the grave just as naked as he was born.

But isn't this true of everyone? It is easy to fall into the acquisition trap. Acquiring things makes us feel good about ourselves. It clothes us in possessions, as it were. But when we die, all of those beloved acquisitions must be left behind. And at that point our nakedness is revealed.

Why does acquisition bring so much pleasure? Is it because it makes us think we have gained something? Is it because acquisition is rooted to some degree in identity? If so, then acquisition is another example of trying to fill a hole that cannot be filled with anything but life.

Adam and Eve were perfectly happy to be naked in the garden until shame came in through sin, bringing the realization that they would "surely die." The deep meaning of the story is that death is our nakedness and shame and the cause of all our sorrows.

All sorts of coverings are put on in an attempt to conceal this nakedness. Fashion is an obvious example. Riches and fame are coverings. A career can be a covering. So can academic degrees. Even sports and hobbies are often used as coverings.

What all these things have in common is that they are *exterior*. They are not ourselves; they are something we put on. Solomon is reminding us that anything we put on in our quest for contentment—anything—at some point will be ingloriously stripped away.

The Great Reduction

Look what I have seen: it is good and comely for one to eat and to drink, and to enjoy the good of all his labor that he undertakes under the sun all the days of his life, which God gives him: for it is his portion.

If riches cannot make us happy, then what in the world can?

Now Solomon circles back to the reduction he has been staggering toward throughout the book. And here he makes it plain again that he is not glorifying work or simple pleasures for their own sake. He is glorifying them because of God, who gives them.

Epicurus recommended seeking tranquility in the pleasures of the stomach because he believed that matter is all there is. Solomon says we should enjoy them because they are gifts from a benevolent Creator. We are not sure how these two ideas become confused, but they are very different.

The contentment Solomon is recommending in eat and drink and work is based on *gratitude*, for these good things come from the hand of God. But what kind of gratitude can there be in Epicurus, who does not believe that God made the universe or is in any sense provident?

Solomon is wiser than Epicurus because he understands that gratitude is the key to contentment. If we roast a delicious turkey, we can certainly find pleasure in it and a full stomach, but not happiness. Gratitude graces the roasted turkey with something that cannot be found in it for its own sake.

Evidently the person commended here is the poor laborer who has sweet sleep. The idea of his contentment may be especially poignant to Solomon because of the great crimes he has committed. He has not only accumulated wealth and wisdom, but he has also led Israel down the fatal path of idolatry.

The poor laborer is incapable of achieving the great things Solomon has achieved, but he is also insulated from any such gross malfeasance. His lowly status has shielded him. And perhaps his innocence has something to do with his ability to enjoy what he has.

Here's a strange irony: the lowly laborer has the grace of God, the very thing for which Solomon is fruitlessly striving. God's graciousness shines especially on the poor.

The Great Reduction

Every man also to whom God has given riches and wealth, and has given him power to eat and to take his portion and to rejoice in his labor; this is the gift of God. For he shall not much remember the days of his life; because God answers him in the joy of his heart.

In a sense the entire book has been about power; specifically, what has the power to make us happy? Solomon has gone through a long list of things, all the usual suspects, and concluded that none of them have this most highly-desired power *in themselves*.

In the preceding verse we have a picture of the contentment of the simple laborer with his simple pleasures, as Solomon imagines it, but here we have a picture of potential contentment even in a wealthy man, *if* he has the power to eat and take his portion and enjoy his labor.

The word "power" here, or *dominion*, is usually taken to mean that he is the master of his riches and is not enslaved by them. If we contrast this example with the one that follows, we might also conclude that it is *within* his power to enjoy them; i.e., no one can take them away from him.

A very different kind of power also comes to mind, however—the power to find contentment in what we have and enjoyment in our work. It is one thing to have riches and wealth, but it is quite another to be able to enjoy them.

Solomon has everything, both riches and high-profile labors, and the mastery of wisdom, and yet it seems he lacks the power to be content with them, to be at peace. But what good are they to him if he lacks this all-important power and finds himself tossing in his bed at night?

He may actually wind up envying the poor laborer who has very little but seems content with his lot. The most important thing is not to have riches and wealth but to have the power to enjoy them; to have contentment. Otherwise they become a source of torment.

By this unsanctioned interpretation what really matters is not what we have or what we achieve but the grace of God, who alone gives us the power to be content with what we have. No one can give himself this gift. This is not something even a super-achiever can achieve.

The Great Reduction

We tend to think of power in terms of strength. So, for example, to have power is to be able to move that stone in our back yard, or tell someone else to move it. But what if we think of it as the power to enjoy? To have riches and wealth and lack this power is worse than not having them at all.

Solomon is a man in deep torment. He has riches and wealth in abundance, and his labors include the mighty temple and palace and three books in the Bible as well as many psalms. But he is not at peace.

Happy are those who have the power to enjoy what they have.

The Great Reduction

> *There is an evil which I have seen under the sun, and it is common among men: A man to whom God has given riches, wealth, and honor, so that he wants nothing for his soul of all that he desires, yet God does not give him the power to eat thereof, but a stranger eats it: this is vanity, and it is an evil disease.*

And this is the contrasting example of someone who has these things and does *not* have the power to enjoy them. Now in the literal sense it seems to mean that someone—a stranger—has taken them away from him. He does not have the power to enjoy them because someone overpowers him.

And again, it could simply mean that the things that he owns overmaster him, as many of the commentaries aver. It is impossible for riches, wealth or honor to give us contentment if we are slaves to them. Solomon has already told us that he who loves silver cannot be content with silver.

But we still wonder if it might also mean that he lacks the power to enjoy them at all. He has them but is simply unable to enjoy them. After all, this describes Solomon himself. He has all of these things and yet he is not content. He has made his unhappiness very plain.

If so, then Solomon has concluded that happiness depends entirely on God. To some God gives the power of enjoyment, and it is a source of contentment; while others, including Solomon himself, seem powerless in this sense, even if they are the king and wisest men in the world.

He has them and does not enjoy them, but then he dies and a stranger comes along and enjoys them instead, perhaps because there is no son to inherit. The thought of the *stranger* alienates us from our riches. It adds to our misery by undermining identity.

The Great Reduction

If a man begets a hundred children, and lives many years, so that the days of his years be many, and his soul is not filled with good, and also that he has no burial; I say, that an untimely birth is better than he. For he comes in with nothingness and departs in darkness, and his name will be covered with darkness. Moreover he has not seen the sun, or known anything: this has more rest than the other.

But what if a stranger *doesn't* inherit? What if this man who can't enjoy what he has does have sons—a hundred of them—and moreover lives many years? If his soul is not filled with good, or the power to enjoy what he has, then those many sons and years simply multiply his misery.

Now again, this could easily be Solomon. The Bible records only four offspring, but a man with seven hundred wives could have hundreds of legitimate offspring. Children were even more ardently desired in the ancient world than today. As Rachel said, "Give me children, or I die."

The reason was not just the natural love of children but the fact that children perpetuated one's memory. Children clothe the shame of our nakedness, but in this case the sufferer's memory is not perpetuated because he has no burial. His children did not avail him at all.

In any case we now see what this is all about. Solomon longs for *rest*. He longs for peace and does not have it in spite of all his riches and wealth and famous labors and multitudinous children. If a man has a hundred children and no burial, then there is no rest for him in those children.

But in what sense would Solomon have no burial? In the sense of an honorable one. His sins were many. Here is an unnerving sample: "Then did Solomon build a high place for Chemosh, the abomination of Moab, in the hill that is before Jerusalem, and for Molech, the abomination of the children of Ammon,"

Molech is the Canaanite god associated with child sacrifice. Perhaps this has something to do with why we don't hear about Solomon's other children. But our point is that a man who builds a shrine for such a detestable god and for such utterly detestable practices cannot have an honorable burial.

Solomon has riches and wealth and perhaps a hundred children, but he is not going to have an honorable burial. It is too late for that, and entirely his own fault. This might help us to understand why his misery is so great that he envies a miscarriage, which at least has no pain.

The Great Reduction

Yes, even if he lives a thousand years twice over, yet has seen no good: for do not all go to one place?

And now we have the same man from the same example, only this time an honorable burial is not an issue because he is going to live twice as long as Methuselah—and yet he *still* does not have the power to enjoy the good things he has.

Think about this. Are two thousand years of the kind of suffering expressed by Solomon better than a hundred, or just twenty times worse? It does not matter how long we might live; we all go to one place in the end, we are all mortal, and that is the source of our sorrow.

Solomon is echoing Moses in Psalm 90: "The days of our years are threescore years and ten; and if by reason of strength they be fourscore years, yet is their strength labor and sorrow; for it is soon cut off, and we fly away."

The strength that may extend a given person's life beyond the usual seventy years leads to continuing labor and sorrow. A prolonged life does not necessarily bring happiness; it may simply bring prolonged suffering. Therefore something that seems like strength is actually weakness.

Both Moses and Solomon attribute this suffering to one reason: we are mortal. The labor and sorrow we experience are the product of our resistance to the limitations of our own existence. Viewed in this way, a limit of seventy years may actually be a blessing for some. It cuts their suffering short.

The light of life had not yet come into the world. Without that divine light, this mortal life involves darkness and suffering. If this life is all there is, then truly "all is vanity." All of the things that seem important—that lend light to life—are in reality fleeting and entirely meaningless.

The Great Reduction

All the labor of man is for his mouth, and yet the appetite is not filled. For what has the wise more than the fool? What has the poor, that knows to walk before the living? Better is the sight of the eyes than the wandering of the desire: this is also vanity and vexation of spirit.

This sums up the examples just given by explaining why contentment is so hard to find. Human nature simply will not allow it. Human nature is *appetite*.

All of our labor is for the mouth, in other words to fill it up, but we are *not filled*. If we eat today we must eat again tomorrow. Appetite demands it. This is the literal sense. The figurative sense is that our spiritual appetite is also unquenchable. It cannot be satisfied by anything we do or possess.

Appetite has become a source of weariness and vexation to Solomon. He was a super-achiever, but it does not matter how hard we work or how successful we might be. At the end of it all we discover that appetite still has not been satisfied. And then we become too old to do anything about it.

In this sense, the wise man has no advantage over the fool; none whatsoever. He is no more likely to be filled up than the fool, just as the poor man who knows how to bear himself in company is no more likely to be filled up by his talent for keeping up appearances than the rich man by his riches.

It is good to be content, but appetite sets our souls on fire. The wise man, the fool, the rich man and the poor poseur all have something in common: they cannot satisfy their own appetite. This is demonstrably true. But why? There is no answer in biology or chemistry.

The sight of the eyes is perfect. Those of us who enjoy good vision have the very great and amazing pleasure of seeing nature with absolute clarity. But there is something in us that cannot be satisfied even with perfect vision. There is something that causes our eyes to wander.

The Bible calls this something *sin*. Adam and Eve lived in paradise, but they were not content with being happy. They decided they wanted to be like God, so they wandered from God. In the same way, sin deceives us and causes us to wander from the contentment that is already ours.

The Great Reduction

This is Solomon's diagnosis of the human condition, obtained not from scholarship or dialogue but from his own experience and the burden of mortal life.

The Great Reduction

That which has been is named already, and it is known that it is man: nor can he contend with him that is mightier than he. Since there are many things that increase his vanity, what is man the better?

The identity of "man" has been well-established down through the ages, in fact since God called him *Adam*. No one can break the mold. This means that Solomon cannot obtain the immortal identity he desires by standing out. Each generation is a recapitulation of the last. To think otherwise is vanity.

Who can contend with someone mightier than he? This could mean several things. It could mean that our fellow beings are an impediment to the transcendent identity we desire. We don't always come out on top, and that makes it hard for us to think highly of ourselves.

It could be a personification of death, with which no one can contend. "All flesh is like the grass." This is an important theme in the Bible. It reminds us to be humble. It reminds us to dig a little deeper for wisdom and not seek contentment in showing off.

Most likely, however, it refers to God. If God is sovereign, then what is "man," and what is his desire to contend with God—to make himself "like God," on the pattern of Adam and Eve; that is, to raise himself up? There is no greater vanity or futility than this.

God's sovereignty has already been ruefully invoked in the "seasons" passage. It is possible to try to resist the seasons of life—but also futile. Summer comes and winter comes, as do youth, middle age, and the decline Solomon is now experiencing and will vividly describe in the end.

To resist those seasons is to contend with almighty God. Let's say he made us to be a carpenter, to give us contentment in building things. In that case to refuse to work with our hands, out of pride or simple laziness, is to contend with God and make ourselves unhappy.

We believe the same is true of marriage. The story of God leading Eve to Adam suggests that he chooses our mate for us. Indeed, many feel they have experienced this phenomenon in their own lives. It is of course possible to try to resist God's will, but foolish if what he has willed is good.

This matter of "Who can contend?" is about participating in the eternal. The end of following our own will is the grave; this cannot be disputed. We have been given the opportunity for something better, for finding a different identity and contentment, but we must be willing to wear a yoke.

To be yoked to eternity is to be a stowaway on a grand boat with a grand destination. We cannot possibly afford a ticket for such a journey, but "come, you who have no money; come buy and eat." All we have to do is love God and keep his precepts and let him prepare a cabin for us.

Is free choice abrogated? Not at all. We are still free to see or not see the goodness of God, and free to choose to submit to his good will or resist it. The only thing abrogated is vanity, which wants to contend with God and is unwilling to accept the reality of the human condition.

Think of Jonah's unwillingness to go to Nineveh. He tried to resist, but the divine will prevailed. He was unhappy when the whole city repented, presumably because he wanted them to be destroyed for their cruelty, but God reminded him of the value of life through the allegory of the vine.

Many things increase our vanity—riches, talents, beauty, power. They make us try to contend with God and remake the meaning of "man." But then in what sense are we better off than the beasts, who lack the capacity to reason?

The Great Reduction

For who knows what is good for man in this life, all the days of his vain life which he spends as a shadow? For who can tell a man what shall be after him under the sun?

This is a remarkable thing for the author of Proverbs to say, isn't it? He wrote an entire book to tell us what is good for humankind. But there is a difference between the kind of practical philosophy he described in that wonderful book and what is confounding him now.

There can be no question that if we follow the excellent advice given in Proverbs we will be happier. Our lives will be much better; we will be much more likely to prosper; we'll stay out of a whole lot of trouble; we'll put ourselves in contention for contentment.

But *happier* is not the same thing as the supreme good of *happiness*. Proverbs makes us happier by teaching us to live the right way, according to the light of life. But living the right way cannot give us happiness when we are mortal beings who crave an immortal identity.

It is this difference, between mortal and immortal identity, that is the source of our wandering desire. We can meet many or all of the objectives laid out in Proverbs but still will not have an immortal identity, the genetic memory of which is passed down to us from our first parents.

Let's say we've made a big name for ourselves like King Solomon and are more famous today than our fellow men and women—who is to tell us what will happen in the future when there are other kings and other passions? Nothing is more easily forgotten than today's fame. Nothing.

Let's say we have acquired riches or even wisdom. Aren't they circumscribed by death? Is there someone who can show us what we will be after death and where our riches and wisdom will be then? No such person exists. Our nakedness cannot be covered by riches or wisdom.

Solomon himself might have a particular interest in having someone tell him what will come after death. He has committed terrible sins, and his wisdom has turned to folly through his foreign wives. Will he be famous for his riches and wisdom and industry, or for something much less savory?

So then who really knows what is good for us in this vain life? Should we consult the philosopher, the wellness advisor, the fitness guru, the TV evangelist, our nutritionist? There are no "happiness experts." Anyone who pretends to be one is fooling not only us but himself.

The Great Reduction

A good name is better than precious ointment.

What we have been seeing so far in Ecclesiastes is a process of reduction. Solomon is leading us through the things that are typically believed to be desirable and to provide the good of happiness and showing us that they all fall short of the mark.

But then what is left over from this great reduction? Well, for one thing, "a good name," which is synonymous with identity. In fact a good name is what Solomon has been striving so mightily to obtain all along. It was his misfortune in old age to realize that he had not understood its true value.

We all know what "a good name" is. When certain people are mentioned we reflexively say, "Oh! Such a wonderful person, generous, humble, charitable, kind." But this type of name is unlikely to be obtained through the type of pursuits that Solomon thought would bring him contentment.

A good name cannot be obtained just by being the builder of a glorious temple. Fame can be obtained thereby, but a good name is something quite different from fame. A good name comes about through how we treat others, not how we build up ourselves through our accomplishments.

The Good Samaritan has a good name. The word *good* is right in his name. And its sweet scent is based on charity. The name of Jesus is perfectly scented because he was humble and healed people and laid down his life for his friends. No other name has such a sweet savor.

A good name comes from obedience to God and his law. Why? Because the law is rooted in love, and therefore the law protects and builds up life. "Whatsoever you would have others do to you, do the same to them, for this is the law and the prophets." This is the secret to a good name.

Solomon says the same thing when he tells us how to obtain a good name in Proverbs: "Let not mercy and truth forsake you: bind them about your neck; write them upon the table of your heart. So shall you find favor and good understanding in the sight of God and man."

A good name soothes the soul and is therefore more valuable than precious ointment, which merely soothes the body. There is nothing the soul wants more than a good name for this reason: it reflects the value of life. Solomon had to go down many roads before he realized it.

But is a good name even possible for him now? After all he has done and the stench of his idolatry? It is quite possible to see these words as another statement of regret. Perhaps Solomon has finally realized the value of a good name when it is too late to do anything about it.

The Great Reduction

And the day of death [is better] than the day of one's birth.

Why such bitterness? Could it be because of the impossibility of obtaining a good name?

The day of one's birth is full of joy and possibilities, but possibility and folly and sin have combined in Solomon's life to deprive him of the joy of a good name. Death at least puts an end to the fecklessness of human nature, which turns possibility sour.

Thus from Solomon's point of view the day of one's death is better than the day of one's birth. This shows the depth of his pain. It is almost the same thing as saying he wishes he had never been born. This is not "wisdom" in any sense of the word; it is an outburst, and that makes it personal.

One irony of a life of ambition and achievement is that it does not necessarily lead to "a good name." It can lead to a powerful name, like Caesar's, but this name does not have the sweet scent Solomon has in mind. And he has made things worse by not being faithful to the God he loved.

In fact, Solomon did not obtain a good name. And it seems that at the end of his life he began to realize it. This might explain why he now feels "all is vanity," and it also helps to explain why he has become so completely focused on the great reduction and simplifying his life.

The Great Reduction

It is better to go to the house of mourning than to go to the house of feasting: for that is the end of all men; and the living will lay it to his heart. Sorrow is better than laughter: for by the sadness of the countenance the heart is made better. The heart of the wise is in the house of mourning; but the heart of fools is in the house of mirth.

Solomon's late-breaking recognition of the value of a good name leads him to desire repentance.

To go into the house of mourning in our minds is a reality check. Excessive feasting amounts to nothing. We can use it to distract ourselves and hide our nakedness for a while, but a time will come when we can no longer be self-deceived. And then we will want to mourn.

To go into the house of mourning is to turn away from feasting—in other words, to repent. Feasting and repentance do the same thing. They both relieve the pain of being human. But feasting is for the body, while repentance is for the soul; therefore the house of mourning is better than feasting.

"Blessed are they who mourn, for they shall be comforted." This seems counterintuitive and strange, but the idea is quite simple. God lifts up—blesses—the mourner through his goodness and his promises of life. Meanwhile the lift we receive from feasting is momentary and insubstantial.

We have seen this in the kings of our own time. Some have tried to distract themselves by filling their lives with feasting and carousing and sex. Their lives were a carousel; once they started down this path, it was impossible to get off. Does this describe Solomon in his later years?

And then there is this: "The sacrifices of God are a broken spirit: a broken and a contrite heart, O God, you will not despise." Put aside your rather desperate feasting; repent and return to God. He will come running to greet you with joy, since "he who was dead is now alive."

Feasting is a celebration of mortal life. It is proud. But we humble ourselves when we go into the house of mourning by acknowledging that all flesh is like the grass. By this change we are reminded that God lifts up the humble and casts down the proud and the mighty from their thrones.

Think of yourself at a funeral. You come out of your busy life, distracted and frivolous, cell phone buzzing in your pocket, but you see the sad countenance of the widow and the beloved children and grandchildren and all frivolousness is stripped away. Their sorrow is good for your heart.

Their sad faces cause us to think seriously about our lives and all the foolishness we use to distract ourselves. If the house of mourning is our final destination, then where are we more likely to find peace and contentment? In feasting—or in repentance, sober reflection, and the favor of God?

Now of course this statement represents nothing more (or less) than an authentic moment of repentance brought on by nothingness and shame. Not every day or every moment is made for repenting. Solomon would not have us be gloomy all the time. In fact he will say just the opposite in a minute.

Remember, too, that this is not gloominess just for its own sake but also for the sake of others. To go into the house of mourning and put on a sad face is to put off the pride and insolence that oppress our fellow beings and make the world such an unhappy place.

Still, this moment of repentance is very important for those seeking contentment. Having seen his mortality, it occurs to Solomon that, ironically, the very thing we hate—a house of mourning—is actually good for us. It shows us who we are and causes us to think soberly about our lives.

Something to think about the next time you're sitting at a funeral . . . or a feast.

The Great Reduction

It is better to hear the rebuke of the wise, than for a man to hear the song of fools. For as the crackling of thorns under a pot, so is the laughter of the fool: this too is vanity.

Yes, specifically because the rebuke of the wise may lead to repentance and send us to the house of mourning. Solomon's father knew this better than anyone. If he had not been willing to listen to a timely rebuke, the stench of his name would have become overwhelming.

The rebuke of the wise can be very painful in the short term. It was devastating to David. But short-term pain leads to long-term gain. To see this and consciously acknowledge it requires humility and is a very good example of the wisdom of Solomon.

Meanwhile the laughter of fools at a feast is pleasing in the short term but fleeting, like thorns cracking merrily under a pot, soon to be burnt up. Think of all the laughing going on in the world. We gravitate to it because it seems glamorous and makes us feel lighter, like helium. And then we crash.

We are quite sure that Jerusalem was laughing and feasting right up to the time of the Babylonian catastrophe. Then they went deep into the house of mourning that is Lamentations. But in their sorrow something wonderful was revealed: "Thy mercies are new every morning; great is thy faithfulness."

Sounds like Solomon is going through very much the same transformation.

Surely oppression makes a wise man mad.

Now, this could mean, as the commentators tell us, that a wise man is being oppressed and is being driven mad by the pain of oppression as well as the powerlessness of wisdom to stop it. Or he himself could be the oppressor, in which case he undoes himself through his own cruelty.

We would like to think it has something to do with what has gone before, however. Solomon sees the tears of the oppressed and is driven to distraction. We are reminded of Habakkuk. "O Lord, how long shall I cry out for help and you not hear, or how long shall I cry violence and you will not save?"

But why do the tears of the oppressed drive a *wise* man mad? Why specifically a wise man? Perhaps it is because wise men love to wax philosophical, as Solomon does in Proverbs; and in order for them to wax philosophical and obtain a sweet-scented identity there must be moral order in the world.

In that case, to see the tears of the oppressed is to be deprived of the beloved identity of philosopher and to have one's nakedness revealed. It is not only painful in the sense that he hates to see injustice; it is also painful because it threatens to invalidate his wisdom about how to be happy.

If Solomon is the wise man in question and Solomon is being driven mad by the tears of the oppressed, then this too is personal, and it helps us to understand his state of mind.

The Great Reduction

And a gift destroys the heart.

Solomon is being driven mad by the thought of the oppression that is omnipresent in the world; is he also being driven mad by the memory of gifts he himself has accepted, perhaps in some cases for the purpose of oppression?

Why do we give gifts? Sometimes out of love; sometimes out of self-love. Someone in Solomon's position is constantly showered with gifts. Some of those gifts are truly gifts of love, especially when they come from lowly subjects who cannot expect a reward.

But many gifts to a king, and the most enticing ones, are based on a desire for advantage, and thus to someone else's disadvantage. To accept such a gift destroys the heart, robbing it of all tenderness and pity, as well as its love of justice, its noblest attribute.

This statement of woeful regret seems to suggest that Solomon has accepted many.

The Great Reduction

Better is the end of a thing than the beginning of it:
and the patient in spirit is better than the proud in spirit.

Which was Solomon, patient or proud? The beginning of a thing is full of giddy excitement and hope, but the end of a thing, the completion, requires patient endurance.

Think of his temple. It was started in great excitement, great joy, but it did not come to fruition in a day. It required careful labors and collaboration and problem-solving. And as we know, with any great project the human element can lead to many challenges.

We are not told about the challenges involved in building the temple, but we know they were there because we have seen them in our own lives and endeavors. Even modest building projects in our local churches can lead to trying circumstances.

But then what about the construction of a magnificent temple, the centerpiece of a national identity? Imagine the disputes, the power-struggles over what should be done and how. Imagine the missteps and suffering as solutions were sought and abandoned for overcoming them.

The end is better than the beginning because the beginning is nothing and the end is something. But in order to make something of value, we must have patience. And patience comes through faith.

The Great Reduction

Be not hasty in your spirit to be angry:
for anger rests in the bosom of fools.

This can tie directly into the previous verse through impatience, which is the source of so much of our anger when we are trying to get things done. Impatient anger is counterproductive. It does not help us to get where we want to go.

If this is what Solomon has in mind, then the deep wisdom of the saying is that any great thing we may be trying to accomplish requires a process that accommodates human frailty. Anger shortchanges this process through impatience, leading to a less satisfactory result.

In any case, it is obvious that anger is the opposite of peace, which is what Solomon is seeking; therefore anger is foolish. And if God is working things out according to his own inscrutable purposes, then anger is also self-defeating. Anger is rebellion against God and his perfect will.

Hasty anger should not be confused with holy wrath. God is angry in the Old Testament when his chosen people violate the law of love; i.e., when they love false gods or do harm to their neighbor. The ground of divine wrath is love, but hastening to anger has selfish reasons.

The Great Reduction

Do not say, What is the reason that former days were better than these?
For you do not enquire wisely concerning this.

In other words, don't waste your time pining for the "good old days." Nostalgia is generally misguided and may embitter us and deprive us of contentment.

We have a tendency to romanticize the past. The reason is that we are unhappy in the present and unwilling to see the real reasons. We may be tempted to blame our unhappiness on the foibles of the age, but people in general have never been less unhappy than we are.

The good old days weren't so good when they were living through them. It is impossible to name a single period in American history when happiness reigned and all were content with their lot. No such time ever existed for a country that began in turmoil and revolution and wanderlust.

Personally, we may be inclined to look back with fondness on a time when, say, Beethoven and Austen and Wordsworth were all alive, creating their pastoral dreamscapes, but the nineteenth century was a dark and uncertain period, as an agrarian past was being cast aside for industrialism.

Nor should we look for a golden age of religion. There were times in Israel's own history when apostasy was so widespread that the prophets despaired of finding even a remnant that remained faithful to God. The same has been true in our own past. There were many times when the churches were empty.

Ironically, Solomon was offering this advice at the very time Israel was in fact enjoying its golden age—during the combined reigns of him and his father. But then this shows that in every age we have a tendency to be nostalgic about the past.

To live in the past is to forfeit the good things God gives us in the present. The morning skies, the scent of a flower, the wholesome food on our table, the children that make life merry, good friends, right worship—they are no less present today than they ever were.

Contentment involves making up our minds to enjoy what we have right now instead of mooning over how happy we might have been if we

The Great Reduction

lived at some other time. This is the proper use of philosophy, by the way: to promote happiness by talking us out of our illusions.

The Great Reduction

Wisdom is good with an inheritance: and by it there is profit to them that see the sun. For wisdom is a defense, and money is a defense: but the excellency of knowledge is that wisdom gives life to those who have it.

Which is more desirable—wisdom or an inheritance? Which one can make us more secure?

We might be inclined to long for an inheritance without giving much thought to wisdom. An inheritance is an obvious defense against want. Those who have money have power, and not just for buying; that is why we are so enamored of it.

But as Solomon reminds us, wisdom is also a defense, first of all against ourselves. Wisdom defends us against false notions, overreactions, foolish schemes, empty ambitions. Wisdom helps us to remove the sting from the disappointments we experience in life.

We recently heard of a couple who won $350 million in a state lottery. Nothing has changed. They still live in the same house and drive the same cars. You would never know they were rich. They give generously not just to their synagogue but to all the churches in town.

Their sudden wealth did not destroy them, as it has so many. This is what Solomon means by an inheritance with wisdom, which is needed in order to make money truly profitable.

Most of all, however, wisdom gives what money cannot give, and that is life. This is a reminder that life is our highest value. Wisdom gives life not on its own accord but by helping us to see the light of life. For Solomon, this light is seen in God's law, which teaches us to do no harm to our neighbor.

Wisdom helps to understand that "the law is spiritual." It is not there to take away our fun but rather to preserve and build up life. When we see this through wisdom, we learn to love God's perfect law; and the first psalm tells us that to love the law and obey it as much as we are able is to have life.

Eternal life? No; this cannot be obtained through the law. But more abundant life? Absolutely. God's law is rooted in love, a constructive power, and those who cherish and obey it will have a more constructive life and a better chance of obtaining peace than those who follow the selfish law of nature.

The Great Reduction

We could provide many proofs and examples, but we are sure you understand our meaning. God's law builds up the lives of others and also our own life—by discouraging us from doing harm.

The Great Reduction

Consider the work of God: for who can make that straight, which he hath made crooked?

But here's the thing—we have nothing to boast about if we love wisdom and God's law. We cannot make ourselves straight. The glorious light we perceive in the law is life, but we are mortal beings. "Thy word is a light unto my feet," but David often stumbled.

The young Solomon was determined to make crooked things straight—to obtain perfection by the law—but in Ecclesiastes he is a deeply chastened man. After all, he has done things in his life that were not straight. He has learned that no one is perfect. He has learned about human frailty the hard way.

Adam and Eve were made straight, but through their rebellion all of their sons and daughters have become at least a *little* crooked. Contentment depends on understanding this very, very clearly. Otherwise we will never make peace with others—or ourselves.

Crookedness is baked in. It is impossible to tune a poorly-made piano to make heavenly music because the instrument itself will not allow it. And it is impossible to tune ourselves to our own standard of perfection because life is our light and we are mere mortals.

First, such wisdom teaches us not to judge others. "Sinful was I from the moment my mother conceived me." This is as true of us as it is of everyone else. Just as we desire others to be tolerant of us and our foibles, so wisdom teaches us to be tolerant of others.

Second, such wisdom teaches us not to frustrate ourselves with perfectionism, as Solomon did. It is impossible to straighten out others just as it is impossible to make ourselves straight. We have to know what we can change and what cannot be changed if we want to have peace.

The Israelites, falling short of perfection, tried to make themselves straight through the sacrificial system. Today we have been made straight through one holy sacrifice. Speaking on a purely personal level, nothing is more essential to peace than knowing this.

In the day of prosperity be joyful, but in the day of adversity consider: God has set the one over against the other, to the end that man should find nothing after it.

The consoling wisdom here is for those who are going through bad times. God provides prosperity to gladden us and sends or allows adversity in order to chasten us and keep us humble. "He hastens and chastens, his will to make known."

Solomon's take is that God has set the one against the other in order to prevent us from being able to predict what will happen in the future. The idea is that he is teaching us to trust in him and his daily bread, which is the only way to overcome the crookedness mentioned in the previous verse.

If that crookedness stems from wanting to usurp God, from the very first sin, then the only way to overcome it is to put aside rebellion and trust wholly in God for contentment and identity. Adversity is the tool God uses to open our eyes to this truth.

Solomon does not promise us a way to *avoid* adversity and suffering. He assumes it will come. But he provides a view of adversity that deprives it of some of its sting. He gives us a way to practice the art of contentment even when we experience adversity, as all do.

He also reminds us not to be ungrateful when adversity comes. "The Lord giveth and the Lord taketh away." If we are pleased to receive good things from God, then it is rather churlish to be angry when things do not always go our way.

"Give thanks in all things," if peace is what we desire.

The Great Reduction

All things I have seen in the days of my vanity: there is a just man who perishes in his righteousness, and there is a wicked man who prolongs his life in his wickedness. Be not over-righteous; and do not make yourself over-wise: why should you destroy yourself? Be not over-wicked, neither be a fool: why should you die before your time?

At first blush this sounds like the problem of theodicy, or why bad things happen to good people. But Solomon has something a little different in mind.

It has occurred to him that the formula for prosperity and long life he proposed in Proverbs should not be overdone. Sometimes it is not the righteous who live and prosper or the wicked who experience destruction. Sometimes the reverse is true.

This leads Solomon to give advice not found anywhere else in the Bible—do not strive to be over-righteous. The commentators think this means don't be so overly zealous that we do ourselves harm. We might add: don't be so overly zealous that we fail to enjoy the good things God has given us.

A little wine and a little company are not to be scorned. Loving the Lord our God with all our hearts and souls and minds includes enjoying the very good things he has made. It is possible to be so overly righteous that we deprive ourselves of the enjoyment of these things.

Now the advice not to be over-righteous does not include the moral law. There righteousness is demanded. But over the long years Solomon has observed an amusing irony—an ascetic lifestyle may lead to premature death while some indulgence may lead to long life.

Solomon is talking about common sense. Anyone is capable of seeing the irony he describes and coming to the same reasonable conclusion; for instance, when we see the centenarian who assures us that the key to long life is a daily glass of brandy and some chocolate.

This advice may go against some of our notions of religion, but as Jesus said of himself, "The Son of Man has come eating and drinking; and you say, Behold a glutton and a winebibbler, a friend of publicans and sinners."

Sounds like Jesus and Solomon might be on the same page.

The Great Reduction

It is good that you should take hold of this and also from this not withdraw your hand: for he that fears God shall come forth of them all.

The preceding ruminations lead to a striking new thought: sometimes it is good to hold onto contrary ideas; or in this case, to not being over-righteous and at the same time not being over-wicked, all the while being guided to safe harbor by the fear of the Lord.

This important concept might do our modern Christians a great deal of good, if they were familiar with it or took it to heart. Jewish wisdom, the deep thinking of the rabbis that we see in Ecclesiastes, is not always "either/or," like Greek philosophy; quite often it is "both/and."

Aristotle gave us the principle of noncontradiction. If two things contradict each other, then only one of them can be true. We see this notion played out too often in our doctrine, for instance in the endless discussion of faith versus works, or predestination versus free will, or mercy versus justice.

But in the rabbis' way of thinking, the principle of noncontradiction does not always apply, because "God's thoughts are higher than our thoughts." This is the way of thinking that Solomon seems to endorse when he says it is good to hold onto the one without letting go of the other.

For example, Jehovah is absolutely transcendent, the creator of the entire universe, and yet at the same time he comes in person to Abraham and makes him a wonderful promise. He is both immanent and transcendent. Noncontradiction need not apply.

Meanwhile philosophy is hopelessly divided over this very question. Is the good of happiness absolutely different from existence (transcendent) or somehow embodied in existence (immanent)? It is impossible to overcome this divide if the good is intellect, as the philosophers believed.

But in the Bible, God is love. Moses encountered God in a burning bush. The bush was on fire, but it was not consumed (both/and). Moses was told to take off his shoes because he was standing on holy ground. God's love is holy and absolutely set apart, but it is also as close to us as our own bare feet.

The Great Reduction

Christ is a little like the burning bush—holy, yet living among mortals without consuming them. He is true God and true man. This both/and doctrine is very important. Because he became true man he can understand us; he knows our weakness and can advocate for us, as we learn in Hebrews.

Are we justified by faith or by works? Paul emphasizes faith; James includes works, as do John, Peter, and Christ himself. If we cling to faith or works, either/or, noncontradiction, we become divided. Solomon's wisdom may unite us by inviting us to hold onto the one without letting go of the other.

The Great Reduction

Wisdom strengthens the wise more than ten mighty men in the city.

For example, the wisdom just articulated about holding on to the one without letting go of the other.

One way such wisdom strengthens us by making it possible to maintain good relationships with people whose views are very different from our own, including family, friends, coworkers, and fellow citizens. It enables us to see the value of their views without abandoning our own.

In the same way, it strengthens the church immensely. We are all very different people with very different notions of value. Solomon's wisdom helps us to find the "unity of the Spirit" where the world and the devil and our own natures are all working very hard to drive us apart.

We are inclined to fall in love with the idea of ten mighty men, ten heroes or champions, because ego and identity cause us to confuse might with right. The beloved figures of the past were mostly martial heroes, and this is still true today. Might is more beloved than wisdom.

We see it in movie after movie. Our hero gets into a dust-up with the bad guy and then subdues him after a mighty struggle. We love watching this fairy tale over and over again because it ties our longing for identity into our lust for domination. But the truth is that might very often is not right.

It is wisdom that shows us this truth and gives us an opportunity for contentment by weaning us from our love of might and domination.

For there is not a just man upon earth who does good and does not sin.

Might cannot be right if no one does good and does not sin. If we are selfish and vain by nature, then we cannot give ourselves the righteous identity we desire by overpowering our foes. Wisdom shows us this truth—and therefore wisdom is needed for contentment.

All stories that do not reflect this unflattering view of human nature are false and misleading. The Bible is not a book of superheroes. God did not allow the Israelites to conquer the promised land themselves. No Achilles or Aeneases are glorified in the book of Joshua.

Instead, God was the one who did the conquering, as he makes very clear. Might cannot be right unless it is God's might because "only God is good." Only God's might can give us contentment, the promised land. Only God can conquer the grave, which is the hidden source of all our sorrow.

If there is no one who does good, then where in the world is contentment to be found? Not in the might of mortals. The mightier they are, the more they will be inclined to do evil. It is foolish to put our trust in heroes like Samson because heroes have feet of clay and will always disappoint us.

Nor can we entrust happiness to ourselves. We cannot satisfy our own standard of righteousness if no one does good and does not sin. We must look elsewhere for contentment, perhaps to a loving Father who is willing to sacrifice his only Son for our sake.

Also take no heed to all words that are spoken, lest you hear your servant curse you. For oftentimes your own heart knows that you likewise have cursed others.

Why? Because "no one does good and does not sin." Those who desire peace of mind would do well not to be too inquisitive about what the world is saying about them. We know others are likely to be catty about us because we love to be catty about others. Cattiness is part of our makeup.

Human nature almost compels us to try to lift ourselves up at someone else's expense. If we were truly good then we would never think to say anything catty, because to be good is to do no harm to our neighbor. To be good is to have life as our light, but we stumble around in darkness.

This advice is important and makes it into the book because the book is about peace and contentment. The thing that drives our unease is identity. This same unease drives all the jostling for identity seen in the world, the contentiousness that is right out in the open in the realm of politics.

If you are a Republican or a Democrat you broadcast cattiness about your opponent that most non-politicians have the sense to keep private. But then to survive in politics, you must have thick skin. In some sense, you must literally not hear the things that are being said to destroy you.

This is even more true of those of us who do not have thick skins and are not angling for political power. If we want to be content and sleep at night and have peace, we would do well not to be too curious about what others are saying. Our little bubble is a good thing.

The Great Reduction

All this have I proved by wisdom: I said, I will be wise; but it was far from me. That which is far off, and exceeding deep, who can find it out?

What he really means: "Why am I still so unhappy?"

We moderns know all about "far off and exceedingly deep." We are confronted with this phenomenon every day. The more advanced our measurements become, the more we encounter certain essential marvels and mysteries at the center of being.

We see "though a glass darkly," not just in science but in the more esoteric realm of wisdom as well. God is good, but then why is there so much suffering in the world? Solomon has already hinted at the anguish this question causes him; he will have more to say later on.

God is good, but then why does someone who loves God die of a ravaging cancer, while others who have little thought of God or the good live long and seemingly prosperous lives? This is a mystery that has plagued inquiring minds from the beginning.

What about cancer itself? God's creation is "very good," and yet we see something astonishingly good, like the body's ability to form new blood vessels in crisis, angiogenesis, turned into a plague that destroys the body and causes much pain and suffering.

Why should children be born with an extra chromosome or deaf or deformed? Surely there is something God can do about that. Why would a family that loves and reveres the Lord be subjected to the misery of having a child who suffers with cystic fibrosis?

Solomon also has more personal questions, such as how can I be the wisest man in the world and still be unhappy, and why does it seem impossible for me to get a good night's sleep? For those living with such intractable burdens, wisdom may seem far off indeed.

The Great Reduction

I applied my heart to know, and to search, and to seek out wisdom, and the reason of things, and to know the wickedness of folly, even of foolishness and madness.

Solomon knows wisdom is far off because he has been trying very hard to obtain it—to see deeply into the reason of things.

Why the "wickedness of folly"? Because folly is the opposite of the identity sought in wisdom. Those who seek to be wise need a foil, and their foil is folly. But Solomon has already seen that the wise man is just as susceptible to the grave as the fool.

Note his interest in understanding madness. Does he mean the madness he has seen in others, or does he have something a little more personal in mind as he peers into old age and his own imminent demise? There will be more on this interesting subject later on.

The Great Reduction

And I find more bitter than death the woman whose heart is snares and nets, and her hands as bands: he who pleases God shall escape from her; but the sinner shall be taken by her.

What has he gained from all his striving and searching for wisdom if he can clearly see those snares and nets and still finds himself entangled in them, over and over again? Just how powerful is wisdom when feminine wiles can render him powerless?

He has a lot to say about this in Proverbs, and sometimes it is quite searing: "For she hath cast down many wounded: yea, many strong men have been slain by her. Her house is the way to hell, going down to the chambers of death."

Sounds a bit personal, no? Perhaps a man who loves nothing more than to consider himself wise has found that he is no match for a woman whose heart is snares and nets. This happened to Solomon when he allowed himself to be seduced into idolatry.

Paul confessed that the good he intended to do he did not do, while the evil he was determined not to do—that was the very thing he did. Why? Because it seems there is "another law" at work in him, the law of sin and death, against which wisdom is sometimes powerless.

Because of this law, it is not *wisdom* that can save Solomon from the snares that he fears, but only the grace of God. Such women exist, just as destructive men exist, but only he who pleases God will escape them. He has found from personal experience that wisdom does not have this power.

Now it must be said that Solomon, by his own account, brought down many, many women. To be used once and put into a harem is to receive a life sentence where there can be no intimate marital love and no family circle. So perhaps he should not be casting the first stone.

But at the same time, he has become the "sinner" in his own example. Not only has he been beguiled by a woman whose heart is a snare—or more likely by many among his wives—but he has allowed himself to do the very thing he was warned against from the beginning.

As Paul said, "Who will rescue me from this body of death?" Only God through his grace. It is the grace of God that is glorified in Solomon's lament about the power of women to make fools of wise men. Compared with that, wisdom is nothing, as he has learned through experience.

And this, too, puts wisdom in its place.

The Great Reduction

Behold, this have I found, says the preacher, counting one by one, to find out the account—which my soul still seeks and does not find—one man among a thousand have I found; but a woman among all those have I not found.

More is not better. Solomon boasts of his seven hundred wives and three hundred concubines, but here he adds them all together and concludes that there is not one like the Shulamite in the entire harem, one who loves him truly and whom he truly loves.

This is the fate of kings. They cannot be truly loved in the way Eve was made for Adam. It is very difficult or impossible for a king to become "one flesh" with his queen. Power arrangements stand in the way. If this is true of one, then it is a thousand times true of a thousand.

Don't blame the women. They cannot love Solomon the way Eve loved Adam for the very reason that he is a king. If there are a thousand women in the harem, then the harem is an inherently political organism. One flesh cannot be divided a thousand times.

The man who is one flesh with his wife is made whole and has a bulwark against the madness of existence. Christ himself said that two become one flesh, although he was unmarried, and sanctioned the institution of marriage with his first miracle.

This very high conception of marriage is reflected in Solomon's own Song of Songs, essentially a love song. Unfortunately the Shulamite, his nut-brown maid, was not enough for him. He added 999 to the one, and the sum turned out to be zero.

Is this misogyny? We tend to think of it more as an expression of bitter regret. In the end he will conclude that a good wife is the most important element in happiness. But here he laments the choices he has made, which have made him proud but not happy.

His reference to "one man" reminds us of his father's deep friendship with Jonathan, which meant "more to him than the love of woman." But he too was a king, or destined to become one, and he too married for political reasons, including Jonathan's sister.

The kind of friendship David and Jonathan had is a wonderful thing, to be sure, and much to be cherished, but it cannot compare with the mystery of becoming one flesh.

The Great Reduction

> *This only have I found, that God has made man upright;*
> *but they have sought out many new things.*

As is shown by having a harem of a thousand. God has given us everything we need to be happy, but instead of studying to be content with what we have we have gone in search of new things.

Solomon proclaims this is the *only* thing he has found in his search for wisdom. In that case, it is the core insight of the book. Our unhappiness cannot be blamed on others, least of all on God. We bring unhappiness on ourselves because of our wanderings.

God made men and women very good. When they fell from that goodness and became mortal, he gave them his law as their light. But instead of doing what God told them to do they did the kinds of things described by Solomon, none of which can lead to contentment. And they did worse.

This shows that rebellion is at the core of human nature. God gives them all good things, but they cannot be content with this goodness. They want to be like God. They want to be lifted up and glorified. Therefore they go in search of many schemes.

God made Solomon upright in wisdom and warned him against foreign wives, but Solomon went in search of a thousand new things. This sorrowful lament could easily be about himself.

The Great Reduction

Who is like the wise man? Who knows the interpretation of a thing? A man's wisdom makes his face to shine, and the boldness of his face shall be changed.

The commentators seem to see this as praise of wisdom, or even glorification. In that case, the sense would be that wisdom causes the wise man's face to shine by changing the hardness or "boldness" that may be otherwise etched there into gentleness and humility.

But since Solomon doesn't actually say this, it occurs to us that it may also be about the *limitations* of wisdom. He was a wise man whose face shone until he realized that his wisdom could not save him from feminine wiles. And then his boldness of his face was changed—he was humbled.

We don't know if Solomon is in the mood for glorifying wisdom. He has been engaging in a reevaluation of the thing he loves the most. He has discovered that there are limits to what can be known. He has discovered that wisdom cannot answer questions like why bad things happen to good people.

Wisdom cannot dry the tears of the oppressed. Wisdom cannot help us to sleep on our beds at night or give us peace. Worst of all, wisdom, it seems, cannot save us from ourselves. Solomon was wise, and yet he succumbed willingly to his foreign wives.

There can be no doubt that wisdom is commended by Solomon and highly cherished, but if we think we are wise—if we are puffed up with our wisdom and made bold—then we are fools, because the "wisdom of men is foolishness to God" and "there is no one who does good."

James says the wisdom that comes from God is pure, peaceable, gentle, easily entreated, full of mercy and good works, impartial, without hypocrisy. In other words, not at all puffed up. In that sense, it is quite the opposite of what the world expects or sees in those whom it considers wise.

"Who is like the wise man?" is a rhetorical question. The implied answer, we suspect, is no one. Solomon may be thinking of his own pretensions. He may be thinking of his egotism and the pleasure he took in having famous people like the Queen of Sheba seek him out as the wisest man in the world.

At one time his face shone with his wisdom, but now his boldness has been changed. This is in fact the story of the entire book. His wisdom did not save him from horrific folly. It did not prevent old age and decline. Worst of all, it did not make him happy.

The Great Reduction

I counsel you to keep the king's commandment, and in light of the oath of God. Do not be hasty to go out of his sight: do not stand in an evil thing; for he does whatever pleases him. Where the word of a king is, there is power: and who may say to him, What are you doing? Whoever keeps the commandment will feel no evil thing: and a wise man's heart discerns both time and judgment. Because to every purpose there is time and judgment, therefore the misery of man is great upon him. For he knows not what will be: for who can tell him when it will be?

Solomon's rumination on the limits of wisdom leads him to consider the tyranny of kings. We don't think it is so much the purpose of this passage to give practical advice to courtiers as it is to show how weak wisdom is in certain situations; to encourage us to desire God's grace more than wisdom.

The situation described brings people like Boethius or Thomas More to mind. An absolute ruler cannot be controlled by his counsellors, no matter how wise or well-meaning they might be. The Wheel of Fortune raises courtiers up and then remorselessly dashes them to the ground.

The absolute ruler is like a live wire, full of deadly energy and unpredictable. It is impossible to know what sort of violent whim or change might come over him on any given day. There is no hope or true security in his service. There is only the day and its dangers.

Israel was warned not to desire a king. He will take your sons and daughters and turn them into servants or worse. He will take your harvest and use it to wage wars. He will tax you to make himself and his favorites rich. He will take a tenth of your flocks and make you slaves.

This is the devil's bargain we make when we invest our hopes and fears in one fallible man. If we give a sinner godlike power, we create an all-powerful sinner. His whims, no matter how foolish, become our iron rule. There is nothing left but to submit.

In the presence of a foolish king, wisdom has no pride. Indeed, wisdom is often compelled to hide itself, lest it be tempted to advise the king and reap destruction. In some situations no one is in more peril than the truthteller. Poor Kent, he should have kept his mouth shut.

The new CEO gathers lieutenants around him who support his "vision." It is of little benefit to be wise in such an environment. Nothing can be said to stop some foolish program or direction in which he and his minions have invested their careers and bonuses.

Actually wisdom can be dangerous in such situations. The court of the absolute ruler or CEO is no place for righteousness, justice, forward thinking, or even simple honest feeling. It is a place for submission and, where necessary, dissembling. "The misery of a man is great upon him."

Solomon has a unique perspective on this, being a king himself. Did he play the impetuous tyrant and ruin the career and life of some well-meaning courtier—or more likely many? Is there remorse in the advice he is giving?

The Great Reduction

There is no man that has power over the spirit to retain the spirit; neither has he power in the day of death: and there is no discharge in that war. Neither will wickedness deliver those who are given to it.

This goes with the observation that to every purpose there is a time and judgment. No one knows how God is moving in any given situation. It is not wisdom that can save the courtier from the king's destructive whims but only the grace of God, which is shed on those who please him, like Daniel.

Here we see Solomon's apprehensiveness about death descending on him again. Wisdom is powerless in the face of such a relentless foe. No one can command the Spirit, the Lord and giver of life, not even a king. When the time comes, his spirit will depart.

Nor is there any discharge from the war that is death, as there is from other wars (Solomon makes a little joke here). Everyone must fall. The wicked at court will not be able to deliver themselves through their wickedness. Death reigns triumphant over human pride.

A long time after Solomon it became possible to say, "O death, where is thy sting? O grave, where is thy victory?" The unrelieved gloom he feels as he contemplates his own demise has been turned into joy for those who put their faith in Christ.

But Solomon had no such consolation or hope. In his time it was not clear what came after death, not even to faithful Jews. He gives us an honest account of the effect of death on the human psyche. Its honesty sets him apart from the philosophers.

In our day, there is a conspiracy to hide the dislocation and darkness that descend upon the soul with the thought of death. The enemies of faith, our own proud Epicuruses, want us to think they are carefree and happy. But will identity allow us to be satisfied with annihilation?

There is this strange irreducible thing in us called the "I." It stands starkly in our grammar, and everyone seems to know exactly what it is. It has an immutable quality; every day it wakes up the same. Science cannot explain it. There are no "I" molecules.

What is it, then? No one knows. It is real, but we do not have any idea of why it exists. It is this "I" that is enshrined in identity. Solomon has become aware of it in an uncomfortable way because of his unhappiness and inability to change his situation.

This "I" is the light in our being as long as it has life. But death snuffs out this smoldering wick. Is it really possible, then, to make peace with death? Or does the thought of death plunge us, like Solomon, into deep gloom and darkness?

The Great Reduction

All this have I seen, and applied my heart unto every work done under the sun: there is a time in which one man rules over another to his own hurt.

Just as riches can hurt a rich man, so power can hurt a powerful man. Solomon is that man. He has not been the good and gracious king he wanted to be. His wisdom has not enabled him to obtain the identity he desires.

Adam reflected God's image in the sense that he was made the master of creation just as God is the Lord of all being. His sin was to try to make himself like God and lord it over his fellow beings through the power of judgment.

We all think we want to be in charge. It's simple human nature to believe we can do better. Solomon has been a king and a judge most of his life, a man with absolute power. But these words indicate that sometimes he has found it to be to his own hurt.

To be the lord of others requires great wisdom and even greater humility. For one thing, we must be willing to listen to our wise counselors, even if their advice gives us pain. When Nathan comes to us we must hear him and turn from the path of destruction.

It seems likely that at least one of Solomon's many advisors must have been brave enough to counsel him to avoid foreign wives. After all, they had many opportunities, and they had the scriptures. Were well-meaning courtiers punished, perhaps even killed, for giving this good advice?

Was Solomon at any time during his long reign a little like Henry VIII, punishing those who foresaw the unhappy outcome of his desire to turn relentlessly from one woman to another? If so, then he punished them to his own harm and marred his own identity.

Now of course we are just speculating that this is what Solomon has in mind, but there are countless examples of how the love of domination can lead to our own harm, not just at court, but also in the church, or business, or politics, or in any walk of life.

It was one of Shakespeare's favorite subjects. The problem is we are sinners. We cannot rule in righteousness; we are no better or more capable or godlike than Solomon or David. Thus the vanity of wanting to lord it over others leads to our harm.

Wisdom counsels us to be wary of our love of ruling. If we desire to do some good with power, then this is a motive to be praised. But power makes good motives go awry.

The Great Reduction

And so I saw the wicked buried who had come and gone from the place of the holy, and they were forgotten in the city where they had done so: this is also vanity.

Solomon notes the strange case of kings or rulers who were wicked but had an honorable burial. We ourselves know of a municipal building named for a magistrate who molested young women. We suspect there are many such monuments in the world, even in churches.

Even so, they were forgotten in the city where they were judges and magistrates. They were buried with honor, because of their position, but no one remembers them. Solomon may have his own wickedness in mind. If so, it is poignant that "this also is vanity"—the honorable burial, that is.

An honorable burial, the thing so ardently desired in the ancient world, is meaningless if even wicked men can have them, as we know happens all the time. Solomon himself may have an honorable burial, but he has acted dishonorably. Therefore he can take no comfort in it.

Even an honorable burial is vanity, because in time these wicked kings were forgotten in the city. We should have no trouble understanding this; all we need to do is consult our own history, although we call our kings "presidents." Almost all of them are forgotten.

The Great Reduction

Because sentence against an evil work is not executed speedily, therefore the heart of the sons of men is fully set in them to do evil.

This could simply be a practical observation about kings and kingship—or Solomon could be laying the groundwork for the very troubling question that's about to be raised: why do good things happen to bad people?

God is patient with us. He does not immediately step in and punish wickedness, and therefore we go right on sinning. To put it another way, God gives us the *freedom* to sin, and we gladly take advantage of it. Solomon simply says "the heart of the sons of men." He does not make any distinction.

This could explain why the wicked seem to prosper. God is showing forbearance. It is not that their sin is condoned or their identity approved; instead, God is giving them a chance to turn from their wickedness and repent. Good things happen to bad people because God is merciful.

But this forbearance might also apply to Solomon. He can see the divine rod of punishment after the fact, as he looks back on his life, and may wish it had fallen on him earlier and stopped him from doing evil. And in that case these words may be an expression of deep sorrow and regret.

Solomon has engaged in a great deal of wickedness. He may be expressing a wish that God had not waited until he was an old man to punish him with conviction and remorse but had applied the rod earlier and stopped him from involving himself so deeply in sin.

Think of his father. It was bad enough that he committed adultery with Bathsheba, but then he made things far worse by arranging for her husband to be killed. He might have wished that God had shown him his sin earlier and at least saved him from blood guilt.

But on the other hand, Solomon may simply be talking about the duties of a king, in which case the meaning is very straightforward. Human nature will tend to evil if it is not checked. Governments are put in place by God to punish wrongdoers and protect the innocent.

The Great Reduction

Though a sinner do evil a hundred times, and his days are prolonged, yet surely I know that it will be well with them that fear God, that fear before him: but it will not be well with the wicked, and neither will he prolong his days, which are as a shadow; because he does not fear God.

As a continuation of the previous thought, if punishment is withheld then a sinner may do evil a hundred times.

Solomon is reassuring himself here—and us. We all see sinners doing evil a hundred times and causing pain and destruction to us and to others. We see it in government, in the workplace, and in our own private lives, and it is frustrating.

Now of course this is real life. This is part of our suffering. We build our identity on fearing God, and to fear God is to fear his holy wrath; but then what about all those people who do not fear God and do not seem to suffer any negative consequences?

What Solomon says here, then, amounts to a faith statement. It is not a matter of what he sees with his eyes; his faith tells him that the wicked will not prolong their lives. And in the end it will go well with those who fear God.

Contentment depends upon faith. If we go by our eyes, we are likely to make ourselves very unhappy by what we see in the world. But faith is the "substance of things not seen," and faith gives us the great gift of contentment by putting justice into the hands of almighty God.

Solomon has *chosen* faith. This choice lies before us every day. We should be grateful. Those who do not love God may not have this choice. And for them, contentment is impossible.

The Great Reduction

There is a vanity which is done upon the earth; that there are just men to whom it happens according to the work of the wicked; again, that there be wicked men, to whom it happens according to the work of the righteous: I said that this also is vanity.

Again, why do bad things happen to good people? And maybe even more troubling, why do good things seem to happen to bad people?

Why do the just experience misfortunes that seem to belong to the wicked, while the wicked appear to prosper and be blessed—that is, to enjoy the rewards that seem due to the just, according to the justice narrative that we all have in our hearts and is part of our identity?

Solomon feels the same painful uncertainty we all feel when this thought assails us. It does not matter that he is the wisest man in the world. His philosophy does not shield him from the unsettling realities that sometimes threaten to overturn our applecart.

In fact, no one can answer this question. We have too high an opinion of ourselves if we think we can. An entire book of the Bible is dedicated to it, and this is how God responded in the end: "Where were you when I laid the foundations of the earth?"

In other words, God's thoughts are not our thoughts. It is presumptuous to question God's justice (see Malachi)—but it is also presumptuous to attempt to justify God; to rationalize, like Job's friends, as shown by the sharp rebuke they received.

The fact that bad things happen to good people contradicts the justice narrative seen in Proverbs, and Solomon undermines his own identity by now admitting that this narrative seems to have some holes in it. Hence the frustrated outburst—"This also is vanity."

Solomon staked his identity on wisdom, but *one little question* has felled him. Wisdom, then, cannot give him the identity or the contentment he desires. Wisdom is a high but limited value; and he will expand upon this theme at some length as we go along.

The Great Reduction

Then I commended mirth, because a man has nothing better under the sun than to eat and to drink and be merry: for mirth abides with him due to labor the days of his life, which God gives him under the sun.

His frustration with hard questions drives him to recommend a merry heart. Again, this is not Epicureanism, since the days in which there is opportunity to be merry are described as a gift from God; and mirth is connected with labor, not pleasure, which is a different kind of wisdom.

It is also important to understand that these words are a *reaction*. They do not stand by themselves; they are a rueful response to the deep pain caused by the thought of the vanity of wisdom when faced with the world's most troubling questions.

Solomon is commending mirth as an antidote to the sorrows of wisdom. Rather than striving to be wise—and often making ourselves miserable—we might be better off to labor happily with our hands and enjoy the food and drink and companionship that God has given us.

After all, Christ loved a good dinner party. He turned water into wine when the supply was running low. He made breakfast for his disciples at the seaside after the Resurrection. No one should dismiss these mirth-giving things lightly if they were not scorned by the Son of God.

The Great Reduction

*When I applied my heart to know wisdom and to see
the business that is done upon the earth:
(for also there is he that neither day nor night sees sleep with his eyes).*

He continues on the subject of the limitations of wisdom. The parenthetical insertion applies to himself. He is the poor fellow who cannot sleep either day or night. His sleeplessness is the torment that led to his comment about the rest of the laborer being sweet.

This can be seen as an explanation for his previous statement. It may seem foolish or reductionist for a wise man to say there is nothing better than to merrily enjoy the work and food and drink God has given us. But now he tells us why he said it:

The Great Reduction

Then I beheld all the work of God, that a man cannot find out the work that is done under the sun: because though a man labor to seek it out, yet he shall not find it; furthermore, though a wise man think to know it, yet he will not be able to find it.

In short, wisdom is impossible. There are many things that exceed our grasp. This is a crushing realization for someone who chose wisdom as the thing he desired most. Solomon's identity literally falls apart. No wonder he can't sleep at night.

The simple question of why bad things happen to good people has undone him, as it has many who claimed to be wise. Job's friends made fools of themselves trying to answer it. Others choose to follow the cynical advice of Job's wife and curse God or question his existence.

Solomon is caught in the middle. As we have said, he is definitely not a scoffer. The expression "all is vanity" is not meant to imply that there is no God and no divine justice. Instead, it means there are some things no one can understand, and it is vain even to try.

"Though a wise man think to know it." There are definite limits to what wise men and women can know. This is true in the realm of science, and it is also true when faced with such questions as why bad things happen to good people.

Solomon's love of wisdom can become a form of idolatry. The forbidden fruit seemed desirable to Eve because of its power to "make one wise." A connection was established from the beginning between vanity and the desire for wisdom.

She created a living hell for herself by tasting that desirable but deadly fruit. She obtained the exalted prize of wisdom only to realize that she was naked, that she was the creature and not the Creator. Her nothingness was revealed to her, and this is a nakedness that cannot be covered up.

The same thing has happened to Solomon. The pursuit of wisdom, far from making him happy, has become a source of sorrow in his old age. The harder he tried to clothe himself in wisdom, the more he realized how naked he really was.

This isn't the way it was supposed to be. Proverbs says exactly the opposite. Solomon has changed. He no longer believes that wisdom can make him happy.

For all this I considered in my heart even to declare all this, that the righteous, and the wise, and their works, are in the hand of God: no man knows either love or hatred by all that is before them.

Tortured as he is by Unanswered Questions, by his own inadequacy, by the seeming injustice in the world and oppression, Solomon now consoles himself with the thought that the righteous and the wise are in the hand of God after all.

What they see before them—bad things happening to good people and good things happening to bad people—as painful and discouraging as this might be—is not the ultimate reality. We cannot see the love or hate of immortal God clearly in things that are happening right now in this mortal realm.

There is another layer to reality that is beyond our vision and comprehension. This layer is the eternal one. It is impossible to know exactly how God is working in the lives of people we know. What may seem to us like inexplicable suffering may in fact be redemptive in ways we do not understand.

And what may look to us like the triumph of the unjust may actually be their undoing. All we see is their laughing faces. We do not know what kind of emptiness lies behind the mask, just as we do not know what judgments God might have in store for them. We base our opinions on appearances.

"The Lord disciplines the one he loves." Things that cause us pain in the present may be for our own good in the long run. By the same token, it is implied that God may *not* discipline the ones he does not love. That may be the reason for those laughing faces.

The Great Reduction

All things come alike to all: there is one event to the righteous, and to the wicked; to the good and to the clean, and to the unclean; to him that sacrifices, and to him that does not sacrifice: as is the good, so is the sinner; and he that swears as he that fears an oath. This is an evil among all things that are done under the sun, that there is one event unto all: and yes, the heart of the sons of men is full of evil, and madness is in their heart while they live, and after that they go to the dead.

Are we feeling him yet, this most unhappy man?

This is not Solomon the confident moralist speaking. It is not his goal here, as it was in Proverbs, to tell others what to think and how to live their lives. Nor is he a scoffer. Solomon in his dotage is not a cynic living in his barrel or cold-hearted philosopher by any means.

No, this is a man in pain. The "one event" is death. All men and women are in the hands of God, who has appointed a limit to their days. On one hand, this may seem comforting, because it means the blasphemers will have to face their maker in the end, no matter how things may appear now.

But on the other hand it is not so comforting. It means the good and the devout will also die. Solomon himself will die, and in fact it is his sudden awareness of his mortality that has sent him into his present tailspin. His great works? His riches? They will all pass to another.

Here we see the difference between Solomon and Epicurus, who claimed it was possible to push the shadow of death out of our minds through pleasure. Solomon tried that, and his continuing anguish suggests that no such thing is possible. You can judge for yourself which view is more realistic.

His pain makes him frank. "The heart of men is full of evil." This is not the way we want to see ourselves. If true, it would seem pointless to ask why bad things happen to good people. If our hearts are full of evil, then the more interesting question is why a holy God does not simply wipe us out.

It is also pointless to put our faith in human wisdom, in philosophy. We are unlikely to obtain peace through the work of the mind, as Plato and Aristotle claimed, if our hearts are full of evil. The reason Solomon cannot find peace through his wisdom is that the instrument itself is darkened.

"There is madness in the hearts of men while they live." This statement makes Ecclesiastes a book of great pathos. If Solomon's long complaint is an attempt to fend off madness, then its harshness is not what it seems. It comes from the fear of his own unraveling and sleepless nights.

He has already explained this madness to us. We are held together by stories; otherwise it would be easy for us to fall apart—for instance, when we become aware that bad things happen to good people and see the tears of the oppressed. The stories that hold us together are sometimes quite brittle.

And there is also evil in our hearts, "another will at work in our members." This innate darkness drives us out of the light, forcing us to come to terms with our limitations. "O wretched man that I am!" Paul says in desperation when he sees his own lack of spirituality. This is close to madness.

If our hearts are full of evil and there is madness in our hearts, then wisdom cannot save us. Solomon needs to look elsewhere for peace.

The Great Reduction

For to him that is joined to all the living there is hope: for a living dog is better than a dead lion. For the living know that they shall die: but the dead do not know anything, neither have they any more reward; for the memory of them is forgotten. Also their love, and their hatred, and their envy, is now perished; neither have they any more a portion forever in anything that is done under the sun.

Do you have that rare friend who tells you the truth? Such friends are invaluable. In order to move forward in a productive way, we must know the truth about ourselves. Our friend risks alienating us by being a truth-teller, but he is also being true.

Solomon is being just such a friend in these verses. We may not like what he has to say, but there's no denying it is true. And by the same token we know the world is not our friend because it never tells us the truth like this. The world is too busy stoking our illusions.

True medicine begins with an accurate diagnosis of the disease. In this case Solomon has explained our disquietude. We may not consciously think these things, but they are present to us in the dim recesses of our minds. We know perfectly well we are naked.

Go through the passage statement by statement and decide for yourself if there is any falsehood in it. "Their love and their hatred and their envy is now perished." This is not what we want to hear because these things are precious to us; but we know he is right.

The things that seem so vivid and real to us right now—every conflict, every passion, every painful exclusion—will perish and simply cease to exist. This helps us to put such things into perspective. There is no point in clinging to things that vex us and make us unhappy when they will soon pass away.

The things that may seem big to us now actually begin to seem quite small from the eternal perspective. The purpose of pursuing such a perspective is to give ourselves respite from our troubles; to give us peace. It helps us see that maybe we shouldn't love our love and hate and envy quite so much.

The Great Reduction

Solomon also acknowledges his nothingness. This is not the faux nothingness of our modern sages, which is nothing more than an attempt to make themselves look like heroes through resistance to concepts of being. No, this is true nothingness, where *all* of our illusions are lost.

Nothingness can be the start of a new somethingness. If we are not happy with the way things are now, if we are as restless as Solomon in all of his striving, then maybe we need to clear the decks and start fresh, unencumbered with old baggage, and rethink the way we are doing things.

Also it is not until we truly know we are nothing and have gone into our darkest place that the glory of God becomes fully apparent to us, like sun breaking through the clouds. Therefore Solomon does us a service by telling us the truth about ourselves.

The Great Reduction

Go your way, eat your bread with joy, and drink your wine with a merry heart; for God now accepts your works.

Solomon annihilated himself in the preceding verses and his identity as a wise man, embracing his nothingness and evil heart and even madness. This is bitter medicine, hard to swallow, but it is also liberating. Having tumbled into nothingness, he is now in a position to rise.

Everything that has no value has been stripped away, including even the memory of him, which is the last vanity of all. And *then* comes the great reduction. Eat your bread with joy and drink your wine with a merry heart. The simple tangible goodness of such things is a remedy for your unrest.

God now accepts your works for the very reason that you have been knocked down flat. When we are no longer laboring for glory, we lose the burden of attempting to justify ourselves. Work can then provide a release from our madness instead of making it worse.

The Great Reduction

Let your garments always be white; and let your head lack no ointment.

These white garments represent the joy discussed in the preceding verse. They represent purity, freedom, cleanness, new beginnings, freshness, a blank slate. We feel moved to observe, however, that the garments are *put on*. The person underneath has not changed.

There is no departure with this admonition from the essential sadness of the narrative. Indeed, a new kind of sadness has been introduced by acknowledging that the peace and contentment so desperately desired must in some sense be put on.

This act is admittedly superficial. It is not as though Solomon can actually make a clean start or give himself joy by putting on white garments. He cannot hide his own cover-up from himself. He knows better than anyone that the white garment is put on.

But while he cannot be that clean, white thing, he can find some joy in the representation of it. In the same way, he may not be the person who is able to find mirth or contentment in meat and drink and labor, but there is joy for him in representing this contentment.

And yet, and yet . . . these verses do mean exactly what they say. It is indeed possible to make a fresh start in our minds, to reset. Solomon has gone deep into the depths of sorrow and even madness, but it is still possible to use the power of the mind and reason to lighten the load.

To that end he gives us some specific advice. Let your head lack no ointment. This reminds us of his father: "He anoints my head with oil, my cup runs over." The ointment represents the anointing we receive from God through his grace, the oil that brings joy and refreshment.

The ointment makes our heads feel fresh and clean in a hot and dusty climate. It is not a new start, but it is a *representation* of a new start, a representation we make to ourselves in our minds. Although the power of the mind to change our circumstances is limited, we should not dismiss it.

Put on white garments because they make you feel better. We might remember that the idea of white garments makes another appearance much later on. They are worn by the redeemed surrounding the throne of Christ and are white and clean because they have been washed in the blood of the Lamb.

For those struggling with the burdens and sorrows Solomon describes, of sin and our own mortal nature, of evil in our hearts and even madness, there can be great joy in putting on the white garments of redemption in our minds.

The Great Reduction

Live joyfully with the wife whom you love all the days of the life of your vanity, which he has given you under the sun, all the days of your vanity: for that is your portion in this life . . .

Solomon has a lot to say on this subject in sundry places. In fact he wrote an entire book that is, at least on one level, very much a celebration of conjugal love, and very romantic.

Here is some stunning advice from Proverbs: "Let your fountain be blessed: and rejoice with the wife of your youth. Let her be as the loving hind and pleasant roe; let her breasts satisfy you at all times; and be ravished always with her love."

Now *ravished* is a word we see all the time in romance novels, but we probably don't expect to see it in the Bible. It suggests that the good wife is everything to her husband. A great mystery began when Eve was made from Adam. She was taken from his side, and he cannot be whole without her.

"Two become one flesh" because she is of his flesh. God made her from him; and, according to the story, God leads her to him, a suitable companion. This burst of passionate poetry at the beginning of the book is meant to signal something elevated and important.

If two become one, then the loneliness that runs darkly through Ecclesiastes can be remedied to a significant degree. "The wife whom you love" gives shape and meaning to what otherwise may seem like utter vanity. Most men know this is true (we do not presume to speak for women).

Married men in general may take in these words with a sigh. They have such dreams and illusions when they are young. It is not until they grow older, like Solomon, that they learn to appreciate their wives and the company they provide and haven from life's follies.

Here is something they may only admit to themselves: they do not like it when their wives go away, because then the madness returns.

The Great Reduction

. . . and in your labor, which you do under the sun. Whatsoever your hand finds to do, do it with all of your might; for there is no work, or scheme, or knowledge, or wisdom in the grave, where you are going.

Now don't forget that Solomon did not have any clear idea of heaven. He did not know what happens after death because this had not yet been fully revealed. It was revealed in signs and figures, especially in the exodus, but not until Christ and the apostles did we have a fuller revelation.

Therefore he counsels us to make the most of the work we have now. This advice may be especially useful to men, who cannot be happy (in general) if they do not have work to keep their restlessness at bay. We do not know if it is equally true of women.

The work Solomon had in mind, in ancient society, would have included things like farming, construction in its many forms, and the crafts: the work of the laborer that leads to sweet sleep. This type of work is satisfying because it has measurable results.

Of course women also were hard workers. They were domestic engineers. There is a famous picture of their industriousness in Proverbs 31. Women who work hard can find contentment in their work, in or out of the home; of this we have no doubt.

The laborer who works with all of his might loses himself in his work. Unhappiness is forgotten when his focus is exclusively on the thing in front of him. Such work brings a desirable identity, since work is respected. It is also redemptive, because to accomplish something is not nothing.

The laborers who work with all of their might show they have submitted to the will of God, who, according to Solomon, prepares their work for them. They are not like the world, which concerns itself primarily with fortune and fame. They are philosophers, in their own way.

The type of work Solomon has in mind produces useful things. The hard-working carpenter makes beautiful and durable homes. The hard-working plumber provides fresh water. The hard-working nurse produces health and comfort. Labor, then, is service.

But then what about labors of the mind? What about lawyers, teachers, etc.? Mental labors may not lead to the sweet sleep that comes from physical exertion. They can bring contentment if we love them, however, especially when they are rooted in service.

This is not theology, by the way. It is philosophy. It is about how to find contentment and peace in everyday life. Solomon is not claiming that anyone can be saved through his works, merely that work can have redemptive value in a practical sense.

The Great Reduction

I returned, and saw under the sun that the race is not to the swift, nor the battle to the strong, neither yet is bread to the wise, or riches to men of understanding, or favor to men of skill; but time and chance happens to them all.

But now Solomon adds an all-important caveat. Do not allow your work to inflame your vanity. Are you fast, strong, wise, smart? Don't get cocky because time and chance happens to us all.

"The race is not to the swift" is one of our favorite sayings. It does not make any sense at all to the worldly mind. Of course the race is to the swift! But Solomon has a very different "race" in mind. The grave conquers all; therefore it is foolish to try to puff ourselves up.

A similar idea is seen in the Beatitudes, where the poor in spirit and the meek, ironically, are said to be blessed. This type of blessing has nothing to do with winning worldly trophies or fortune and fame. It means being filled with God and his love, not with ourselves and our accomplishments.

As for Solomon, there's only one race he cares about now, having grown old. He wants to obtain peace. The attributes that made him a star in the world cannot help him. He describes himself as the wisest of men, the richest, the most accomplished—but then why is he so restless and unhappy?

It is a strange fact of existence that those who are poor but trust in God may be more content than the dynamo living in the gaudy mansion next door. If contentment is what we desire, then faith has more buying power than riches. "Has not God chosen the poor in this world to be rich in faith?"

My mother tells the story of her grandmother, a poor immigrant whose son was killed in a football game back in the days when no one wore helmets. The following Sunday she went to church and forced herself not to cry. She was not there to weep. She was there to drink in the joy of the Lord.

We cannot find what we are looking for—identity—in how swift or powerful we are because these things are not the "I"; they are only accidents of the "I," as we discover in old age when they are taken away. The race is not to the swift because shalom can only be found in God.

The Great Reduction

For man also does not know his time: as the fish that are taken in an evil net, and as the birds that are caught in the snare; so are the sons of men snared in an evil time, when it falls suddenly upon them.

Like the teenaged football player who dies on the grassy field on a fall afternoon, the race is not to the swift because we are all in the hands of God.

This reminds us not to get ahead of ourselves or take anything for granted. We have seen the friend or family member struck down by disaster. Fish and birds are ensnared by superior beings; so too was Job. It would be wrong to think ourselves immune.

Consider the First World War. How many fine young men with bright futures were caught in the net of that pitiless disaster? Or consider the black plague. The sickle mowed everyone down without discrimination: young, old, rich, poor, educated, ignorant, religious, irreligious, heedless, good.

Consider the corporate minions whose company is sold. How will all their hard work save them from the reckoning to come by people who do not even know their names? Consider the sleepy commuter who cannot avoid the panel truck that jumps the divider in heavy traffic. Was it something he did?

If we think about such things seriously, the only sensible response is gratitude for the grace that has been given, as well as recognition that it is vanity to compare ourselves with others.

The Great Reduction

This wisdom have I seen also under the sun, and it seemed great to me: There was a little city, and few men within it; and there came a great king against it, who besieged it and built great bulwarks against it. Now a poor wise man was found in it, and he by his wisdom delivered the city; yet no man remembered that same poor man. Then said I, Wisdom is better than strength: nevertheless the poor man's wisdom is despised, and his words are not heard.

Remember a little while ago when Solomon was assuring us that wisdom was better than ten mighty men in a city?

Still true, but here he confronts the limitations of wisdom head-on. It is quite possible to be wise and also be despised for your wisdom—or worse, neglected. Wisdom, far from always having the signifying power Solomon ascribes to it, can actually lead to nothingness.

Through your wisdom, you may deliver an entire city from destruction, but that does not mean you will be honored. This is especially true if you have the misfortune to be poor. Mortals tend to equate wealth with value; therefore the poor are pushed aside.

Let's face it—Solomon's wisdom was honored because he was the king. He had incredible riches and power. But what about the poor wise man who saves a city? Is the world also impressed with him? Can his wisdom give him the assurance Solomon has been seeking?

Who is honored in our time? The poor wise man, or the rich man, wise or not? Wisdom is better than folly, and wisdom is valuable for its own sake, more so than any precious gem—but it is foolish to think that wisdom will always be honored.

Come to think of it, Christ himself was a poor wise man who saved a city with his own blood. He came with deep and saving wisdom, but was his wisdom honored? Far from it. His wisdom made the Pharisees hate him and was one of the main things that got him crucified.

Wisdom per se does not have the power to give Solomon the immortal identity he is seeking. Wisdom is powerful, and highly desirable for its own sake, but it cannot give him peace.

The Great Reduction

The words of wise men are heard in quiet more than the cry of him that rules among fools.

This seems like a continuation of the same gloomy thought. Wisdom has less power, less effect in the realm of politics than it does in quiet places where human vanity is not so prominently on display. That is, it is least efficacious where it is most needed.

It is safe to assume that Solomon, as king, has experienced the powerlessness of wisdom firsthand. He can offer deep wisdom on pressing issues, but the very nature of politics and organizations guarantees that his wisdom will often go unheard or be undervalued.

True, there is the thing about "fools." Solomon takes some pleasure or solace in pointing out the foolishness of those who ignore his wisdom or wisdom itself. Name-calling is fun. But it provides very little consolation and no shalom.

Solomon's wisdom is renowned; the Queen of Sheba comes to see him for his wisdom. But "a prophet is without honor in his own town." This strange reality forces him to acknowledge that the power of wisdom to provide contentment is limited.

The Great Reduction

Wisdom is better than weapons of war:
but one sinner destroys much good.

Wisdom is better than weapons if it can deliver a city without bloodshed, but it is not always stronger than selfish motivations. The wise king cannot always make things turn out right. There are forces beyond his control that may render his wisdom impotent.

For instance, his wisdom may show him that people in high places are evil or misguided, but he may not have the power to do anything about it. It is a simple fact that one clever sinner can destroy much good in public settings. History provides copious examples.

What if that sinner is naturally charismatic? Or riding on the crest of opinion? Or the ward or protégé of a neighboring king or some powerful noble? In such cases the king cannot attempt to rein him in without putting himself in peril. This shows again the limitations of the thing he loves the most.

Or worse, what if the "sinner" in question is himself? What if he has been a wise man who has now become a sinner? This is in fact what happened to Solomon. And then wisdom turns to shame.

The Great Reduction

Dead flies cause the ointment of the apothecary to send forth a stinking savor: so does a little folly him that is in reputation for wisdom and honor.

The last interpretation might help to explain this bitter outburst. Is it Solomon, the wisest man in the world, who has engaged in "a little" folly and made his reputation stinking? Actually he has shown great and incomprehensible folly by worshiping his wives' foreign gods.

We are human; therefore anyone who seeks identity in wisdom is living on a wire. This is especially true if one is as exposed to public scrutiny as King Solomon. Tongues love to wag, and they will certainly be wagging if the wise king does not live up to his exalted reputation.

What this means is that wisdom cannot save us. It is wrong and foolish to believe it has this magical power. That which is crooked cannot be made straight. We may have all the wisdom in the world, but we cannot make ourselves perfect by our very nature.

When we stumble, our "wisdom" becomes an embarrassment. Far from giving us a desirable identity, our love of wisdom makes us look foolish and conceited. This describes Solomon himself. He was a wise man whom we tend to see today as a man of folly.

If we think of this in terms of trying to get to sleep at night—of the practical use of philosophy, the love of wisdom seen in Solomon—then there may be no greater agony than in knowing that our exalted identity has acquired a "stinking savor."

The Great Reduction

A wise man's heart is at his right hand; but a fool's heart at his left.

Is Solomon the fool who has allowed his heart to be at his left hand in spite of all his wisdom? In practical terms, the wise person favors the stronger hand in politics and indeed in all things. It is foolish to do otherwise. Everyone has weaknesses, but only a fool exposes them.

But this can get very tricky for a king. It is easy for him to find himself in situations where the heart leads him to expose his weakness. For Solomon, the strong hand was the word of God, as he makes plain in Proverbs—and yet his heart led him to seven hundred wives and terrible idolatry.

The heart is stronger than reason, and therefore a wise man may wind up acting like a fool. It sounds like Solomon knows what is right and cannot do it. If so, then this verse reminds us of Paul, and shows us again the limitations of wisdom.

The Great Reduction

Yes and also, when he who is a fool walks by the way,
his wisdom fails him, and he says to everyone that he is a fool.

Now, admittedly, we have wandered pretty far from the commentators, whose insight and linguistic acuity we greatly respect. But it seems possible to us that this section of the book may also be about the idea that "all is vanity"; specifically about Solomon's growing disenchantment with wisdom.

It seems possible to us that these verses all go together. First Solomon admits that sin destroys a reputation for wisdom, then he confesses it is foolish to have favored his weak hand, and now he laments that when a formerly wise man acts like a fool everyone can plainly see he is a fool.

This interpretation fits in well with the bitterness of his remark about a woman whose heart is a snare. At one time he had obtained a reputation as a wise man, but now he has squandered his reputation on beautiful foreign women and made himself to look like a fool.

Not a pleasant thought to take to bed with you on a cold winter night.

If the spirit of the ruler rises up against you, leave not your place;
for yielding pacifies great offences.

Now let's imagine we are in the middle of a story.

This is Solomon's real life. There is someone at court whom he has generally regarded as his "right hand," someone he looks upon favorably. But for whatever reason, this person has somehow become an object of the king's wrath, just as Solomon's father fell into disfavor with Saul.

It does not matter how wise the king may be; over the course of time and changes at court and in himself he will occasionally make the mistake of confusing his right hand with his left and turning against the wrong person, perhaps because of opposition from that person when the king is wrong.

If so, he cannot come right out and say he was wrong. What he can do, however, is advise all courtiers, in a general way, not to desert the court in such situations. He assures them that a yielding spirit compensates for many offenses. In other words, the king will not stay angry with you forever; please stay.

If this is the backstory to this verse, which otherwise seems to drop into the narrative out of nowhere, then it is a tacit admission that the king's vaunted wisdom has failed him, and a plea to his own court to be patient with his shortcomings.

The Great Reduction

There is an evil which I have seen under the sun, as an error which proceeds from the ruler: Folly is set in great dignity, and the rich sit in low place. I have seen servants upon horses, and princes walking as servants upon the earth. He that digs a pit shall fall into it; and whoever breaks a hedge, a serpent shall bite him. Whoever removes stones shall be hurt therewith; and he that cleaves wood shall be endangered thereby. If the iron is blunt, and he does not whet the edge, then he must use more strength: but wisdom is profitable to direct.

Here we have some very interesting advice concerning kingship and folly. Don't try to reinvent the wheel. Don't try to go against old wisdom and do things in a new way, because there is a reason for that old wisdom, and you may find yourself in hot water.

And again, is this possibly about Solomon himself? Are these things he foolishly did, perhaps when he was a young green king, and learned to regret; or worse, when he grew old and sentimental? Is this a confessional statement? If so, it helps us to understand why he cannot sleep at night.

There is a natural order to things. Folly is discouraged in high places where seriousness is expected, and the rich are accorded special honor in the public square as an acknowledgment of their power. Admittedly, these are nothing more than norms, but to defy the norm is to become abnormal.

Hence the folly of servants on horses while the prince walks on the ground. The inversion is tempting because it can show humility in the prince and a new way of doing things. But the problem is that by honoring the servant the prince puts everyone in the place of the servant; i.e., above himself.

The prince may do such things to distinguish himself, to enhance his identity through innovation and thinking out of the box, but the net effect is to undermine his authority as a prince. There are norms associated with being a prince. These norms are not arbitrary but are the outward forms of authority.

True, in themselves these forms are empty. But they are part of the implicit narrative of order in the realm. Defying them may not have the

The Great Reduction

intended effect. The servant who, contrary to norms, is put on a horse above his prince may actually despise his prince for not acting like one.

Solomon points out the foolishness of norm-breaking with a series of humorous proverbs. If you dig yourself a pit by putting your servant on a horse and yourself on your feet, you will surely fall into it. You will become the prince who walks on his feet and is not respected.

Beware of wanting to break through a hedge, because a serpent may bite you. The prince who puts his servant above himself is trying a little too hard to break through the hedge of the norms of kingship. But if you shove your hand through a hedge, there may be a serpent on the other side!

Perhaps the hedge is there for a specific reason, to protect you from harm. Therefore do not be in such a hurry to break through it. And the serpent does not need to be an actual snake. It could be someone at court who sees the foolishness of your iconoclasm and takes advantage of it.

In the same vein, whoever removes stones will be hurt thereby—that is, by the removal. Picture these stones as a wall, and the similarity to the hedge image becomes clear. Walls are there for a reason. Don't be in too much of a hurry to take them down.

But if you really are going to cut down the norms that are in place, then by all means sharpen your axe. Do not use a blunt instrument, like placing your servant above you, or you will make your work harder and your foolishness will be seen.

A king should be mindful of the normalcy of norms; but when he decides that an old tree needs to be felled, that its time has come, he should sharpen his axe, no matter how much longer it takes him to do what he has in mind.

Did Solomon forget to do this? Is this partly why he is so unhappy?

The Great Reduction

> *Surely the serpent will bite without enchantment;*
> *and a babbler is no better.*

That is, the aforementioned serpent on the other side of the hedge. He must be kept in enchantment in order to keep him from biting—for instance, by the norms of kingship, which keep his snake-like striking nature in check, his propensity to ridicule the king.

It is the dignity of the king that keeps this kind of serpent in check, through fear and awe, but the king forfeits that dignity when he puts his servant on his horse. And if the serpent, the crafty opponent at court, will bite with his witticisms, then so will every common babbler.

The Great Reduction

The words of a wise man's mouth are gracious; but the lips of a fool will swallow up himself. The beginning of the words of his mouth is foolishness: and the end of his talk is mischievous madness. A fool also is full of words: a man cannot tell what shall be; and what shall be after him, who can tell him? The labor of the foolish wears every one of them, because he knows not how to go to the city.

More acerbic observations on kings and foolishness. The words of a wise man are gracious because he does not try to glorify himself. He understands that "all flesh is like the grass." He knows that the Lord "scorns the scorners, but gives grace to the lowly."

This grace is the source of the graciousness in the wise man's words. In order to be filled, we must first empty ourselves and be humble. Since God is gracious, to speak graciously is to be exalted. "Whoever exalts himself will be humbled, and he who humbles himself will be exalted."

Graciousness is very comely in a king. There is a reason why "your grace" is a title of high honor. To be gracious in your speech is to exhibit an expansive mind and majesty. It is to put yourself above the fray, just as grace rises above judgment.

Graciousness is shown in an economy of words. This indicates a consciousness of the value of others and their thoughts and opinions. Graciousness is hard because it requires us to remove all private passions. When a king is gracious he shows that he has the greater good in mind.

The fool, however, swallows himself up by talking too much. The more he tries to dominate the conversation, the more he shows how small he is. As a younger Solomon said, "Even a fool, when he holds his peace, is counted wise: and he that shuts his lips is esteemed a man of understanding."

But is Solomon referring to himself? Has he caught himself talking like a fool?

The Great Reduction

Woe to you, O land, when your king is a child, and your princes eat in the morning! Blessed are you, O land, when your king is the son of nobles, and your princes eat in due season, for strength, and not for drunkenness! By much slothfulness the building decays; and through idleness of the hands the house drops through. A feast is made for laughter, and wine makes merry: but money answers all things. Curse not the king, no not in your thought; and curse not the rich in your bedchamber: for a bird of the air shall carry the voice, and that which hath wings shall tell the matter.

A "child" in the sense of being a fool, that is. Building up and maintaining a kingdom requires great industry and wisdom. If we are too slothful to maintain the "house," the realm, then it will decay; if we don't bother to fix the roof it will rot and cave in.

This cannot be done by a childish king who starts the day with feasting and drunkenness. Maintaining the house requires strength, and morning drunkenness takes all strength away. We have a vivid example of this in Ahasuerus, who held a feast for 180 days and made himself weak.

Blessed is the land whose king is a noble son and who feasts with his princes in due season. Not that feasting is inherently bad—but please; not in the morning, not when there is serious work to be done. We are reminded of Hamlet and his frustration with the drunkenness of his fellow Danes.

It is money that answers everything, not feasting. The royal subjects may be made temporarily merry with feasting, but it is the largesse of the king that binds them to him with hoops of gratitude. Therefore do not curse the king or the rich, not even in your private moments, lest you be left out.

Again—is this a lecture or is Solomon talking about himself? Has his own foolish conduct—servants on horses and feasts in the morning—become part of his sorrow and shame? Solomon himself may be the putatively wise man who has done all of these foolish things.

If so, it is not difficult to understand why he might feel that "all is vanity."

The Great Reduction

Cast your bread upon the waters: for you shall find it after many days. Give a portion to seven, and also to eight; for you do not know what evil shall be upon the earth. If the clouds be full of rain, they empty themselves upon the earth: and if the tree fall toward the south, or toward the north, in the place where the tree falls, there it shall be. He that observes the wind shall not sow; and he that regards the clouds shall not reap. As you know not what the way of the spirit, nor how the bones do grow in the womb of her that is with child: even so you do not know the works of God who makes all. In the morning sow your seed, and in the evening withhold not your hand: for you know not whether shall prosper, either this or that, or whether they both shall be alike good.

Following on the thought that "money answers everything": be generous with what you have. Cast your bread, your money, your resources, upon waters and you will find it again. It will return to you. What you give away as a king becomes the source of your strength.

Give a portion not just to one but to seven, the symbol for completeness, or to eight, above and beyond. Why? Because you do not know what evil may come tomorrow, and you do not know what friends you may need when trouble comes.

Is this cynical advice? We see it as practical advice. Actually Christ says almost the same thing: "And I say to you, Make friends for yourselves with the mammon of unrighteousness; so that when you fail they may receive you into everlasting habitations."

The king's treasury is the "mammon of unrighteousness." This is a simple fact. Solomon boasted of all his wealth, but how did he get it? Not by woodworking. Since it has not been obtained in perfect purity, be extra generous with it. This is Christ's counsel and also Solomon's.

You do not know the way of the Spirit. "You hear the sound of the wind, but you do not know where it comes from, or where it is going." You do not know the way of gestation. What happens in the womb is a miracle, no less today than in Solomon's time.

Since you know so little of God's plan, do not attempt to be shrewd with regard to generosity. Do not flatter yourself with studying the wind or the clouds or the seasons. These things are all far beyond you. Do not try to calculate the effects of generosity, because they are also beyond your thinking.

Sow your seed in the morning and do not be stingy. Open up your hands, O wise king, and become a fountain of kindness and generosity to your people, because you do not know which gift will have the most benefit. Let generosity be your rule for its own sake and put aside all calculation.

God desires generosity. He wants the poor to be blessed. Both Christ and Solomon advise the king and the rich to invest their wealth in people. And both use self-interest to encourage them.

The Great Reduction

Truly the light is sweet, and it is a pleasant thing for the eyes to behold the sun: But if a man live many years and rejoice in them all, yet let him remember the days of darkness; for they shall be many. All that comes is vanity. Rejoice, O young man, in your youth; and let your heart cheer you in the days of your youth, and walk in the ways of your heart, and in the sight of your eyes: but know this, that for all these things God will bring you into judgment. Therefore remove sorrow from your heart, and put away evil from your flesh: for childhood and youth are vanity.

Ecclesiastes is the tale of an old man looking back on his life with great melancholy. He has lived in the limelight, but now the days of darkness are crowding in. The light of life shines brightly in youth; in old age it grows dim or goes out.

Not only this, but the days of his gathering darkness shall be many. Oh, how this reality sneaks up and surprises us! Having been accustomed to nothing but light, we must learn to adjust our eyes to darkness and the weariness of mortal existence.

This is the trap in which Solomon now finds himself. He has seen the darkness, the twilight time when he can no longer pretend to be a child of promise. He cannot become young again. He must be what he is.

Therefore he has some advice for young men: take advantage of being young while you still have your youth. This is a gift that is never given again. Do not be old in your youth, and scorn to live in your pleasant illusion, but embrace it.

Walk in the ways of your heart. Do what you love, do not be deterred by the wisdom of old men, such as it is. Rejoice in your youth, for youth is worthy of rejoicing. But do not take your eyes off God. Remember, he will bring all into judgment.

Take sorrow away from your heart, but do not make the mistake of falling into evil, for the days of youth are a vanishing vapor, and all that remains after they are gone is the memory, good or bad, pleasant or painful, of everything you have done.

Who knows this better than Solomon?

The Great Reduction

Remember now your Creator in the days of your youth, while the evil days do not come, nor the years draw nigh when you will say, "I have no pleasure in them"; while the sun, or the light, or the moon, or the stars, are not yet darkened, and the clouds do not return after the rain; in the day when the keepers of the house shall tremble, and the strong men shall bow themselves, and the grinders cease because they are few, and those that look out of the windows be darkened, and the doors shall be shut in the streets, when the sound of the grinding is low, and he shall rise up at the voice of the bird, and all the daughters of music shall be brought low; also when they shall be afraid of that which is high, and fears shall be in the way, and the almond tree shall flourish, and the grasshopper shall be a burden, and desire shall fail: because man goes to his long home, and the mourners go about the streets.

Finally Solomon reveals what he is *really* feeling. We see the source of the melancholy that has oppressed him throughout the book.

Once he was a vital young man, full of promise and light, but now he has grown old, and the light of youth has departed. Yes, it is vanity, this light; yes, it is an illusion in the sense that all men and women must grow old and the light cannot be sustained.

But Solomon, looking back, weeps for the loss of this light. He weeps for his lost youth. It might have been vanity and an illusion, but there was joy in it for him, in all that he did and accomplished, in being a child of promise and living into that promise.

His advice to the departed youthful version of himself, and to all young men and women, is to take full advantage of youth while you can. Don't grow old before your time, because it is certain that your time will come. Do not bequeath yourself regret.

But remember your Creator in the days of your youth. The advice is so important that Solomon feels the need to say it twice. Do the things young people do, but do not forget the one who made you, who is the author of your being and directs your ways and years.

The Great Reduction

The years will come when you will say, "I have no pleasure in them." The years, that is. Your work will be at an end. You will no longer feel the same great joy and exultation at Christmas or at the first snow or the first robin or the mountains or the crashing waves by the sea.

Your friendships will grow a little colder because you and your friends are considerably older. You are not David and Jonathan anymore, vigorous and pleasant to behold. You are wrinkled and gray. Friendship no longer glows with the ardor of immortality.

The sun and the stars are not yet darkened, but they are dim. They do not have the same vivid intensity for you, the pure inspiration, but neither have they gone out. You are still holding onto the light of life, but you also know it is fading. But twilight is not light.

There was a time when sunshine followed rain; when your own moods reflected the weather, and times of dejection were countered by times of sunlight and exaltation. But now clouds follow rain. There is no return of happiness.

The keepers of the house, your own hands, begin to tremble. The strong men that carried you about, your legs, are bowed down. Your teeth cease to grind because they are few. These changes are irreversible. And the decay of the body afflicts the mind.

The eyes that gave light are darkened. The ears that brought joy are shut. You cannot hear the song of the bird that used to enchant you and take away all of your sorrows. The daughters of music that you loved so much—your own songs—they cannot assuage you.

And you shall be afraid. You do not have the strength anymore to protect yourself or the ones you love. Perhaps you never did, but this fact is now brought home to you through physical decline. The high places frighten you, where you used to love to go.

The almond tree shall flourish—that is, your hair will turn white. The grasshopper shall be a burden. When we are young the raucous sound of the grasshopper brings joy because we associate it with life; in old age it grates on us because death is before us.

Desire shall fail, the saddest change of all. Things that used to give pleasure are no longer capable of giving pleasure. It is almost as if desire itself has been snuffed out, the source of youthful joy and happiness. Where has it gone?

"Why are you cast down, O my soul?" Because he must go to his "long home"; that is, his grave. Young men are full of life and do not think about death, but the time will come when death is all they can think about.

The Great Reduction

Or ever the silver cord be loosened, or the golden bowl be broken, or the pitcher be broken at the fountain, or the wheel broken at the cistern. Then shall the dust return to the earth as it was: and the spirit shall return unto God who gave it. Vanity of vanities, says the preacher; all is vanity.

Several metaphors for death, all lined up like pallbearers. The silver cord is life. The golden bowl is all that life holds. The pitcher contains the water of life, which comes, not from ourselves, but from the Spirit of God. The wheel of the wagon is broken at the well; we can no longer carry the water home.

From dust we were made, and to dust we shall return. Life comes from God and returns to him again. Therefore all is vanity that does not honor him, in the strictest sense. The end of the passage reflects the beginning. Remember your Creator, the source of everything good, and of life itself.

The Great Reduction

And moreover, because the preacher was wise, he still taught the people knowledge; yes, he gave good heed, and sought out, and set in order many proverbs. The preacher sought to find out acceptable words: and that which was written was upright, even words of truth. The words of the wise are as goads, and as nails fastened by the masters of assemblies, which are given from one shepherd. And further, my son, by these be admonished that of making many books there is no end; and much study is a weariness of the flesh.

Although we have heard a great deal about the limitations of wisdom, the epiphany that "all is vanity" has not robbed Solomon of his love of wisdom or of making proverbs.

Proverb-making does indeed require acceptable words; that is, "what oft was thought, but ne'er so well expressed." And a proverb must be upright for the simple reason that it aspires to be a proverb. And it must be true or no one will take it seriously.

Put the three together, and you have a very formidable task. Indeed, there is "no end" to the labor Solomon created for himself. If making one enduring proverb is difficult and fatiguing, then making an entire book of them is "a weariness in the flesh."

"Of making many books there is no end" can have an ironic meaning, too. We mortals do love to write books, don't we? And the great volume of books down through the ages, only a tiny fraction of which are still known or read, illustrates that "all is vanity."

And yet Solomon is doing the work God has given him to do. He continues to write proverbs in the same way that a woodworker continues to make tables or a gardener plants his seeds even after a killer frost. And he finds joy in his work.

The words of the wise are like goads—not the soothing murmurs of the philosophers, but hard truths that drive us on to make changes in our lives and attitudes. And they come from one Shepherd: that is, their purpose is to drive us into the fold for our own good.

Ecclesiastes is certainly like a goad. Its purpose is to expose our nakedness and cause us to think soberly about our lives and what is truly of value.

The Great Reduction

Let us hear the conclusion of the whole matter: Fear God, and keep his commandments: for this is the whole duty of man. For God shall bring every work into judgment, with every secret thing, whether it be good, or whether it be evil.

Solomon has ably demonstrated that "all is vanity." Everything that is done in this mortal life is like a vanishing wind; therefore any attempt to obtain contentment by magnifying ourselves is in vain.

"All is vanity" also in the sense that we are motivated by false or incomplete narratives. The comforting ideas we have about things are an illusion. There is oppression in the world. There is injustice in the courts and iniquity in the churches. Good folk are trampled down while the wicked thrive.

The rewards-and-punishments narrative underlying Proverbs does not line up in any neat way with reality. This is not a critique. Proverbs is one of the greatest and most useful books ever written. But Solomon based his identity on that narrative, and it has proven to be fragile.

Proverbs made the writing of Ecclesiastes necessary. The two books are in counterpoise, one relentlessly positive and the other relentlessly remorseful. Either one, by itself, may be too one-sided to present a complete picture of life. "It is good to hold onto the one without letting go of the other."

Proverbs, on the whole, shows us a younger Solomon with all of his dreams intact. It is brimming with the energy and optimism of youth. But in Ecclesiastes Solomon has grown old and seen his own mortality and lost any illusions he might have had about life. This accounts for its bitterness.

In Ecclesiastes we see that a time will come when many of the pleasant flattering stories underlying identity will fall apart and we will realize that all is vanity. Those stories are the thing that keeps driving us forward, our motivation and the engine of success.

If they truly fall apart, then our nakedness is exposed. This has happened to Solomon. At that point there is only one place left for him to go if he still wants a desirable identity: Fear God and keep his commandments, for this is the whole duty of man. The only alternative is "Curse God, and die."

After all vanity has been exposed—the love of silver, of fame, of accomplishments, of pleasure, even wisdom—there is still *something* we can cling to for identity. It is wise to fear God because he holds our lives in his hands. And it is wise to keep his commandments because they give life.

Proverbs and Ecclesiastes are united in their reverence for God's commandments. This reverence is the foundation of the Jewish identity. It is deep because it reflects the value of life, the thing we desire most. And is it enduring because those commandments are rooted in love rather than self-love.

To follow them is to "live a life of love," which is what is left over after all other ways of obtaining contentment have been tried and found wanting. Solomon shows us how he arrived at this conclusion in harrowing detail. His nakedness is a sacrifice that he makes for our benefit.

He has found that God will bring every secret thing into judgment. The reason he is tormented and does not have peace is that he has not loved God with all his heart and soul and mind and he has not loved his neighbor as himself. He has learned to fear God through his suffering.

The conclusion he comes to is not arrived at glibly. He has paid dearly for it with restlessness and sleepless nights and longer days and even madness. And therefore it is more valuable to us.

The Great Reduction

Final Thoughts

Ecclesiastes is about a great reduction—not just the end of the reduction, the refined sauce, but the harsh process of boiling down, shown in discomfiting detail.

It is the perfect book for those who are seeking truth because it tells the truth. In fact it is one of the few books among millions that does tell the truth. It does not permit us to have illusions about ourselves or the significance of our existence.

And why might we be seeking such hard truths? For the sake of contentment and peace. We have a malady, but this malady cannot be cured until we know the real cause; and we cannot know the real cause until we know the truth about ourselves.

The hard truths shown in Ecclesiastes have been revealed to Solomon not because he has grown wise but because he has grown old. The sweet illusions of youth have flown away, and he is left staring at the nothingness of his own vain ambitions.

Thus one vital truth Solomon invites us to come to terms with is that all flesh is like the grass. As much as we might prefer not to think about this truth, it will overtake us in the end. Solomon wants us to know that it is futile to try to hide it from ourselves through over-achieving and pleasure-seeking.

One way this hard truth leads to contentment is through *humility*, which is the opposite of vanity. Pride was the first sin, and humility is the antidote for that sin. "What does the Lord require of you, O man, but to love mercy, do justice, and walk humbly with your God?"

Humility seems to have gone out of fashion these days as we lose touch with our Christian roots and embrace unprecedented wealth and ubiquitous entertainment, the distinguishing marks of the age. It is worth considering, however, because it provides contentment in many ways.

First, to be humble is to be wise. James speaks of the "humility that comes from wisdom." If all flesh is like the grass, then all boasting is foolishness. To be wise is to have a desirable identity, even if the world cannot see it. And this identity cannot be taken away from us, as Solomon's was.

Second, humility reflects the value of life. It not only shows a proper consciousness of our mortal limitations, but it also brings life to others and has healing powers. We refresh the people in our lives with our humility, just as we trample them down with our pride.

Finally, humility realigns us with God, who "opposes the proud but gives grace to the humble." As long as we are full of ourselves, we are like Adam and Eve after they sinned, alienated, alone, and afraid. We cannot have contentment because God is far away. Humility brings God close again.

Ecclesiastes is about being humbled. A superstar grows old and realizes that all is vanity. He has conquered the world but cannot sleep at night. He has a thousand beautiful women in his harem but cannot find one to love him. He has obtained honors and fame but does not have peace.

The depth of his chastening is seen in the declaration that there is nothing better than to live with the wife whom we love and enjoy the work God has given us to do and the food and drink that come from his hands. The common man who understands these things is wiser than Solomon himself.

Beyond humility, the most important takeaway from Ecclesiastes may be that "God has put eternity into the hearts of men." This is what makes it impossible for us to be satisfied with the world or anything in it or with our own accomplishments.

Solomon didn't learn this at university. This realization is the product of his own experience. He was the man who had everything and accomplished everything and found in the end that he was still very unhappy and not at peace. In his frustration he cried out, "All is vanity."

Every year thousands of books are published purporting to reveal the cause of our continuing unrest. Solomon's diagnosis is worth considering because it fits the evidence. If we have an eternity-sized hole in our hearts, then that would explain why we are not at peace in our supersaturated age.

Such a hole cannot be filled by anything we might do or have. It does not matter what we accomplish or how famous we might become or how much silver we might manage to pile up. We still will not have what we are looking for if what we are really looking for is life.

Solomon's solution, for the sake of peace, is the great reduction. Set aside everything that is not essential or life-giving and seek contentment in the good things God has given you, primarily your mate and your food and drink and your labor, and do not forget that God holds your life in his hands.

If vanity is the source of our discontent, then the key to peace is to give up everything that puffs us up and focus instead on the simplest good gifts from God and his life-giving commandments. This seems like very good advice, but we will simply point out that it is still something we must *do*.

Solomon's peace depends on our *ability* to will ourselves to do these things. But there is a peace about which he knew nothing. The peace that passes all understanding can be found by putting our faith in Christ. Why? Because he gives life. He gives us the very thing we want the most.

If the reason we cannot be happy is that God has put eternity into our hearts, then the only remedy for this unhappiness is that God has also provided a way for such a yearning to be filled. He has given us living water that satisfies the thirst for life. All we have to do is believe.

Solomon gives us an honest accounting, based on his own experience and pain, of why we cannot be satisfied with the whole world. But Christ showed us why we can be satisfied with him by laying down his life on the cross. "Greater love has no man than to lay down his life for his friends."

He issues an invitation: "Come unto me, all you who labor and have heavy burdens, and I will give you rest. Take my yoke upon you, and learn from me, for I am meek and lowly in heart, and you will find rest for your souls. For my yoke is easy, and my burden is light."

This is the invitation Solomon was seeking.

ABOUT THE AUTHOR

Jay Trott is an essayist and novelist who lives in the small town of Sherman, Connecticut, with his lovely wife, Beth. Please feel free to contact him at jayatrott@gmail.com.

www.ingramcontent.com/pod-product-compliance
Lightning Source LLC
Chambersburg PA
CBHW071442150426
43191CB00008B/1214